How to patent an Idea

in India

From idea to granted Patent in quickest time, saving costs and making money with your patented invention; a step by step guideline on Intellectual Property Rights

by

Prasad Karhad

Registered Patent Agent in India IN/PA 2352, BE Electronics & Telecommunication

Contents

Acknowledgment

This workbook on patents is outcome of addressing more than 12,000 calls, emails, meetings and visits with inventors willing to file patent for their invention and upon observing their inherent questions from different sectors and background.

A heartfelt thank you goes out to the readers, clients, and followers of patentinindia.com, along with those who have engaged with my articles and videos. Your responses inspires us to strive for excellence and provide the utmost value in each interaction.

I couldn't have done this without help from my mentors in the Intellectual Property and business worlds. A special thanks to my wife, Vaishali, for her inspiration and unwavering support.

I hope you will find immense value in this book, and I trust that this series of information will play a vital role in safeguarding your intellectual property. Thank you for being a part of this endeavor.

Prasad Karhad

Introduction

Dear reader,

This book is most valuable for business owners, entrepreneurs, research and development professionals and working employees who continuously come up with

- Innovative ideas,
- New ways to solve a problem,
- Do research in specific domain,
- New improvements in existing systems to make it more efficient,
- To make system run cost effectively, or
- New and improved way to solve a technical problem of a system

We will start our journey by **defining our end result** that we want to achieve. The outcome expected from Patent protection is,

"We want our innovative ideas and inventions to have broadest possible protection, such that our competitors should not be able to work around our invention without infringing on our patent. We could have complete monopoly over the patented invention in the market and we would be able to monetize this by working on our invention, licensing it to other company to get royalty payments or completely sell the patent rights to other business and get significant monetary benefits for your efforts."

But how can you patent an idea in India? What are the legal requirements and procedures for obtaining a patent in India? How can you ensure that your invention is novel, inventive and useful, and not anticipated by prior art? How can you draft a patent application that covers all the essential features and advantages of your invention? How can you deal with the objections and rejections raised by the patent office during the examination process? How can you enforce your patent rights against infringers and defend yourself against invalidity challenges? How can you exploit your patent commercially and generate revenue from it?

These are some of the questions that this book will answer for you. In this book, you will learn:

- How to go from idea stage to a complete invention disclosure stage
- What is a patent and what are the types of patents available in India
- What are the benefits and challenges of patenting an idea in India
- What are the criteria of patentability and how to conduct a patentability search to identify prior art
- How to prepare a patent application and what are the contents and format of a patent specification and claims
- How to file a patent application and what are the fees and timelines involved in the patent process
- How to respond to the first examination report (FER) and the hearing notice issued by the patent office and how to overcome the objections and rejections raised by the examiner
- How to maintain and renew your patent and what are the annual fees and deadlines involved
- How to enforce your patent rights and what are the remedies and defenses available in case of infringement
- How to license or sell your patent and what are the factors and strategies to consider in patent valuation and negotiation

This book is based on the latest and most reliable sources of information on patent law and practice in India, including the official website of the Indian Patent Office (IPO) , the Patents Act, 1970 , the Patents Rules, 2003 , and the Manual of Patent Office Practice and Procedure . You will find references and links to these sources throughout the book, as well as examples and case studies to illustrate the concepts and principles discussed.

Here are some facts and numbers that support the importance of this book:

1. **India's Growing Innovation and Entrepreneurship**: As one of the fastest-growing economies globally, India is a hotbed for innovation and entrepreneurship. The country's leap in the Global Innovation Index, from 81st in 2015 to 46th in 2021, highlights its rapid progress in these fields.

2. **Strong Patent System**: India's robust patent system, governed by the Patents Act, 1970, and the Patents Rules, 2003, encourages innovation by protecting inventors' rights. The Indian Patent Office (IPO) is dedicated to administering these laws effectively.

3. **Surge in Patent Activities**: There's been a significant increase in patent filings and grants. From 2015-16 to 2019-20, patent applications grew by 17.7%, and granted patents soared by **348.7%**. In 2022, India saw 66.4 thousand patent filings, and 31,261 patents were granted. In 2023, **a record 41,010 patents were granted** as per Minister Piyush Goyal, marking continued growth.

4. **Efficient Patent Processing**: India has improved its patent examination and disposal processes, reducing backlogs. The time taken for the first examination report and patent disposal has been drastically reduced.

5. **International Patent Cooperation**: India's participation in global IP organizations and treaties, like WIPO and the Patent Cooperation Treaty, enhances the international recognition and protection of its patents.

6. **Dynamic Patent Market**: With over 55,000 startups, including 21 unicorns, and more than 4,600 patents filed by these startups, India's patent market is vibrant and dynamic. This environment provides abundant opportunities for monetizing patents.

Financial Year	Patents Filed	Patents Granted
2015-16	43,031	6,326
2016-17	45,444	9,847
2017-18	47,854	13,045
2018-19	50,667	15,283
2019-20	50,659	28,391
2020-21	58,501	30,431

| 2021-22 | 66,400 | 31,261 |
| 2022-23 | N/A | 41,010 (till Dec 2023) |

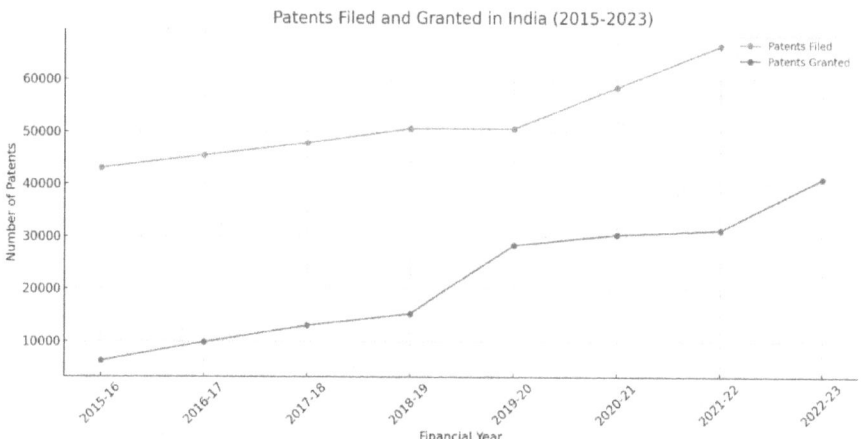

The table shows that the number of patents filed and granted in India has increased steadily over the years, with some fluctuations due to the impact of the COVID-19 pandemic. The patent grant rate (the ratio of patents granted to patents filed) has improved significantly, from 14.7% in 2015-16 to 47.1% in 2019-20. This indicates that the patent office has become more efficient and effective in examining and disposing of patent applications.

Some of **the factors that have contributed to the increase in patent filing and granting** in India are:

1. The government's initiatives and policies to promote innovation and entrepreneurship, such as the Startup India, Make in India, and Atmanirbhar Bharat campaigns, the National Innovation Foundation, and the National Intellectual Property Rights Policy.
2. The improvement in the patent infrastructure and human resources, such as the establishment of new patent offices, the recruitment and training of patent examiners, and the adoption of digital and online platforms for patent filing and processing.
3. The enhancement of the patent cooperation and collaboration with other countries and regions, such as the participation in the Patent

Cooperation Treaty (PCT), the establishment of patent prosecution highway (PPH) programs, and the signing of bilateral and multilateral agreements on intellectual property rights.

4. The increase in the awareness and demand for patent protection among the inventors and businesses, especially in the emerging and high-tech sectors, such as information technology, biotechnology, pharmaceuticals, engineering, agriculture, and more.

5. The development of the patent market and ecosystem, such as the emergence of patent buyers and sellers, patent intermediaries and service providers, patent valuation and licensing experts, and patent litigation and enforcement agencies.

These facts and figures make it clear: Patenting in India is not just viable and advantageous but also crucial for success in today's market. This book will guide you through achieving your patent goals in India, helping you make the most of your inventive ideas. So, if you want to navigate the evolving landscape of Indian patents and harness the potential of your innovations, this book is your indispensable guide.

This book is valuable because it provides you with the essential information and guidance to patent your ideas in India, It offers the knowledge and tools you need to secure, protect, and profit from your patents. Whether you are a novice or an expert, this book will provide you with valuable insights and practical guidance to help you achieve your goals.

The outcome expected from Patent protection

✓ Provide broadest possible protection to our innovative ideas
✓ Competitors should not be able to copy or compete with our invention without our consent
✓ Competitors should not be able to work around our patented invention and build similar solution without infringing on our patent (this is most important point)
✓ we should be able to monetize the patented invention by
  o   by producing patented invention without competition
  o   by licensing it to other company to get royalty payments
  o   by completely selling the patent rights to other business
and get significant monetary benefits for your efforts

---

illustration 1.1

You may be:
- an entrepreneur or a business owner : with an idea or product
- a research scientist : with a new concept, formula to patent
- a Professional or an employee : with new idea for software or ecommerce business
- a ME or PHD holder: with research project
- or a student : willing to learn more about patents

Irrespective of your professional background and field of the invention, the outcome expected from a patent remains the same, "obtaining broadest possible protection to our innovative ideas and making money with your patented invention."

so let's get started with the information that will help you achieve this outcome.

Before we start proceeding, I would like to mention that we are taking a different approach to this important information.

We would be deliberately staying away from the usual educational stuff about intellectual property and patenting invention that is easily available to you. Instead we would be taking **more practical approach**, sometime may be in an unorganized manner yet effective in bringing the value to you.

As this is book and information series is designed especially considering the **your side (inventor's side)** for entire life cycle of the invention and Patent. And all the while we proceed through this information our focus remains on the final outcome (refer illustration 1.1) that we expect from a patented invention.

this book is arranged in

- step by step
- outcome oriented information blocks
- checklists
- and in the workbook format

Where it is specifically designed to guide you through the complicated steps in simple and easy to understand manner to get the best possible outcome with your invention every single time !!!

We will start our proceedings with:

- ☐ defining the objective of this book
- ☐ then we will go through very basis questions you might be having like do I really need patent ? is it worth ? etc..
- ☐ we will see basic definitions and what we can learn from it
- ☐ steps procedure costs involved in getting patent

and we will proceed with details about each step involved that would take you from Ideation stage to granted patent. We will conclude with strategies on making money with your patent and cares to take after grant of patent.

Objective of this book

if this book is to help you with anything...

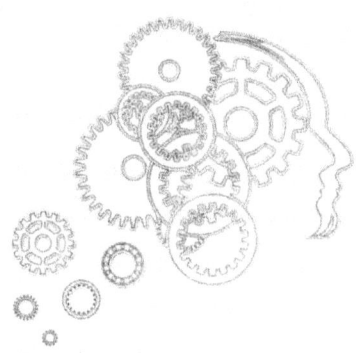

that would be **installing a software in your brain** about the wisdom about patents and building right mindset; a software that will continuously help you in:

- ☐ Spot the opportunities to secure patents for your innovative ideas that are novel, inventive and useful in your field of technology
- ☐ Identify the innovative ideas at the inception level and document them properly in the form of invention disclosures
- ☐ Take informed and speedy actions to file patent applications for your inventions in India and abroad, following the legal requirements and procedures
- ☐ Save costs and time along the way by minimizing mistakes and avoiding common pitfalls in the patent process
- ☐ Ultimately get paid for your patented inventions by utilizing strategies to monetize them, such as licensing, selling, or producing them

And that's why one of the major objective of this book to develop a the **wisdom** and awareness about identifying and protecting your innovative ideas by means of patents.

1. Patent basics, procedure and costs

- Definition of patent and invention, what can we learn from it
- Do I really need to go for patent protection?
  or I should use same money elsewhere (to grow business)
- What inventions are patentable
- What inventions cannot be patented
- Short overview of steps and procedure for filing patent
- Costs involved at each stage
- What would be my contribution at each stage as Inventor

We will start with how patent law defines a patent.

Definition: what is patent?

"A Patent is a statutory right for an invention granted for a limited period of time to the patentee by the Government, in exchange of full disclosure of his invention for excluding others, from making, using, selling, importing the patented product or process for producing that product for those purposes without his consent."

in other words;

"A patent can be defined as a grant of exclusive rights to an inventor over his invention for a limited period of time (generally 20 years from the date of filing of patent application). The exclusive rights are the right to exclude others from making, using, selling, importing or offering for sale his patented invention without his permission."

This implies, when you get patent for your innovative idea, the government gives you a monopolistic right for your invention to stop others from making, using, selling, importing or offering for sale your patented invention without your permission.

What this means in financial terms is you would get significant monetary benefits for your patented invention by:

1. licensing your patented invention to other business and **earn royalties** on regular basis as per agreement
2. you can build a business around your patented invention and stop others from copying it, so there would be no one competing with you with similar product or service, and hence can earn **significant profits**.
3. having patent for your invention may also help in **raising capital** for business
4. You transfer all rights of patented invention to other business. That is make significant money by **selling your patented invention.**

Do I really need a Patent? is it worth the investment?

Table of Contents:

- Do I need Patent? is it worth the investment?
- What if you do not patent your invention
- What if you do patent your invention
- Are patents worth ? deciding whether to file or not ?
- Advantages of getting a patent for your invention
- When deciding if it is worth filing patent
-

Link to video

Do I really need a Patent ? is it worth the investment ?

Well, you think about it all the time, when you are in deciding phase.
- is patent really for me?
- is it really worth the investment?
- what if I don't go for patent and **use that money somewhere else** or in growing my business ?

Fair question, the basic reason behind asking this question is whether you will be able to get the return on investment that you are considering to do for patenting your invention. Now, to answer this in most simplest possible way, let's take an example.

Lets imagine a scenario; you are a business owner or a professional and you are continuously being challenged with different problems in your business on daily basis,

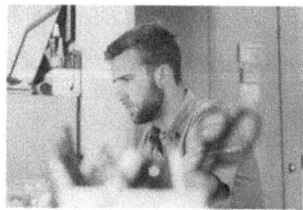

one or the other way continuously challenged
to solve problems

while doing that you happened to come up with an innovative solution for your business

And let's assume **your solution** has real commercial potential in **industry**

The solution has a commercial value in the market. let's go fast forward and your company is successful because you have implemented that solution in your business and you are enjoying the success of that particular solution.

Now, what happened the competitors will jump in and they are there to compete with you.

your competitors **jump in...**

so they will take your product for your innovative solution what you have designed they will **reverse engineer it** and then they will:

- try to beat you on prices
- will try to beat you on quality may be telling a low quality product at cheaper price and
- they probably will try to beat you on scale production

competitors would do whatever the things possible for them to compete and capture your market share. And ultimately even though you are the inventor you are the creator of that solution you have you are the person who first made that innovative idea and worked on it and bring that solution to life, still you end up on losing side.

all efforts that you took goes waste...

and we have seen this happening to business around us, as they came up with some new strategy, innovative ways to do something and every competitor copy that and start competing with them and the progress made again comes back to square one.

All the competitive advantage and potential of making significant profits with your innovative idea goes waste. And you don't have any option but to give in to ever growing competition **and loose**.

Compare this situation with another situation where you have filed a patent application for innovative idea and you got patent granted for it.

Now the situation is different, the competition cannot directly compete with you as patent gives you exclusive rights. "the right to exclude others from making, using, selling, importing or offering for sale your patented invention without your permission" in this case, you yourself can calculate the **return on investment** for your invention.

It is most likely going to be very high potential of profits with your investment in going for patent for your innovative idea, **provided your invention has commercial potential** and you as an inventor or the owner of the invention has the ability and skills required to commercialize the patented invention, and in process make significant money for your research and development efforts.

Another example to illustrate this,

Do you know age of empires ? a mythological game ?

what will happen if a player or kingdom only focuses on financial growth of country and completely ignoring building walls castles and army... ever made that mistake while playing? soon you would be attacked by nearby kingdoms and their army would destroy you. And there is a lesson to be learned from it.

Of course making financial progress and business growth, bringing new clients and more profits is important. However, it is more important **to protect your business** with intellectual properties like patents, trademarks, copyrights, trade secrets etc... which ultimately would be protecting your future profits from the ever growing competition !!!

Not protecting intellectual property of your business would be like building a rich, prosperous country without a defense mechanism or army. It will always be under treat of invasion by other countries (competitors).

Now, all of these examples we have seen from a business owners or entrepreneurs perspective however the inherent advantages and benefits of having a patent for your invention stays the same even though you are a student, working professional or employee or research and development person.

Conclusion:

So, whether to go for patent or not is a decision that should be based on facts and not to be decided on opinions or misbeliefs. Check the commercial potential of your innovative idea and if it looks worth it, then only proceed with patent filing process.

Now, hopefully you got clear opinion about the questions like do I really need a patent or is it really worth it.

Let's consider what are the advantages of getting a patent protection for your invention.

Advantages of having patent for your invention:

Owning an intellectual property has some similarities with owning any other form of tangible property like a real estate. So, what are the advantages of having a real estate property on your name?

- You can rent it
- You can sell it
- You can stop others from using it without your permission
- You can use it for your purpose (business or residence)

on similar terms, patent is an intellectual property and has all the advantages stated above, but you need to claim it to be on your name, hence it is important to file of patent application for your invention. and there is a difference though, unlike real estate the patent has the term of 20 years of ownership.

Advantages of owning patent would be:

- You own exclusive rights for patented invention for given time (20 years from filing of patent application)
- You can use it to build a business around patented invention and not worry about competition
- You can rent it (in this case license the patented invention) to existing businesses
- Exclude others for using, selling, offering for sale and importing your patented invention in India
- You can completely sell the patent to other company

hence this gives a unique advantage to patent owner which can be leveraged for have a complete monopoly and competitive advantage from competition and in certain cases having patent may also help in **raising capital for business** !!!

Imagine what it would be like when:

- ☐ You have exclusive rights for your invention (idea, project, product etc.) and you can stop other from using your invention for commercial purpose for 20 years from filing date.
- ☐ You can make significant return on your investments that you made for research and development and patenting your invention by ways like
  - ○ licensing your patent to other companies,
  - ○ building business around your invention, or
  - ○ completely selling it to other company.
- ☐ You will have better chances of getting funded for your idea, business, product etc. If it is protected by patents, as investors clearly see how they can have monopoly in the market by having patented product for business.
- ☐ You and your business are perceived as an expert in the industry when you have patent. This helps in finding great employees, partners, financers and clients too. Ultimately it enhances your market value.

Indirect benefits of patent

We have seen direct benefits, such as legal protection, market advantage, commercialization opportunities, licensing potential, revenue generation, recognition and credibility, and investor attraction.

However, patenting your invention in India can also have indirect benefits, which are not immediately obvious or measurable, but can still contribute to the worth of your patent in the long run.

Here are some of the indirect benefits of patenting your invention in India, along with some real-life examples and case laws to illustrate them.

Competitor deterrence and prevention of copying of the invention: A patent can deter and prevent your competitors from copying or imitating your invention, as they may fear legal consequences or reputational damage. This can help you to maintain your competitive edge and market share, and to avoid losing your customers or profits to your competitors. However, this also means that you have to monitor and enforce your patent rights yourself, and to be prepared for possible challenges or disputes from your competitors.

For example, in 2017, Monsanto, a US biotech company, sued Nuziveedu Seeds, an Indian seed company, for infringing its patents on the genetically modified cotton seeds, known as Bt cotton. Monsanto claimed that Nuziveedu Seeds had used its patented technology without paying the royalty fees, and demanded an injunction and damages from Nuziveedu Seeds. Nuziveedu Seeds counter-sued Monsanto, alleging that Monsanto had abused its dominant position and charged excessive and unfair royalty fees, and sought a revocation of Monsanto's patents. The case is still pending in the courts, but it has deterred and prevented other Indian seed companies from copying or using Monsanto's patented technology.

Selling patented invention at decent profits because of no direct competition: A patent can enable you to sell your patented invention at decent profits, as you may face no or less direct competition in the market. This can help you to increase your revenue and return on investment, and to create value and gain a competitive advantage in the market. However, this also means that you have to consider the demand and potential of your invention, and to set a reasonable and affordable price for your invention.

For example, in 2014, CSIR, an Indian research organization, licensed its patents on the tuberculosis drug candidates to AstraZeneca, a British-Swedish pharmaceutical company, for further development and commercialization. CSIR received an upfront payment and milestone payments from AstraZeneca, as well as royalties on the sales of the drugs, if approved. CSIR also retained the rights to use the drugs for research and public health purposes in India. The drugs, if approved, would be the first new tuberculosis drugs in 40 years, and would face no direct competition in the market. This would enable CSIR and AstraZeneca to sell the drugs at decent profits, while also addressing the unmet medical need of tuberculosis patients in India and other developing countries.

Establishing yourself or your firm as an expert of the industry: A patent can help you to establish yourself or your firm as an expert of the industry, as it demonstrates your innovative capabilities and achievements. This can help you to attract and retain customers, investors, partners, and employees, and to increase your reputation and credibility in the industry. However, this also means that you have to maintain and renew your patent by paying the annual fees and meeting the deadlines, and to keep innovating and improving your invention.

For example, in 2015, Reliance, an Indian conglomerate, sold its patents on the mobile operating system Indus OS to Google, an American tech giant, for an undisclosed amount. Reliance had acquired the patents from Indus OS, an Indian startup, in 2019, for $58 million. Indus OS was a customized version of Android, designed for the Indian market, with support for regional languages, content, and apps. Google bought the patents to integrate Indus OS features into its own Android platform, and to expand its presence and reach in the Indian market. The deal established Reliance and Indus OS as experts of the mobile industry, and enhanced their brand value and recognition in the industry.

Raising money due to granted patent: A patent can help you to raise money for your invention or business, as it can serve as a proof of concept, a validation of your idea, and a collateral for your loan. This can help you to secure funding from various sources, such as banks, investors, or government agencies, and to overcome the financial challenges or constraints of your invention or business. However, this also means that you have to meet the expectations and obligations of your funders, and to share your profits or ownership with them.

For example, in 2016, Ola, an Indian ride-hailing company, filed a patent application for its invention of a system and method for allocating drivers to customers, based on various parameters, such as location, availability, and preference. The patent application was granted in 2018, and it helped Ola to raise **$1.1 billion** from various investors, such as Tencent, SoftBank, and Ratan Tata. The patent also helped Ola to secure a loan of $156 million from Yes Bank, using the patent as a collateral. The funding enabled Ola to expand its operations and services, and to compete with its rivals, such as Uber and Lyft.

Mortgaging or taking loan on granted patent: A patent can help you to mortgage or take loan on your invention, as it can serve as a security or an asset for your loan. This can help you to access credit from various lenders, such as banks, financial institutions, or government agencies, and to overcome the financial challenges or constraints of your invention or business. However, this also means that you have to repay your loan with interest and fees, and to risk losing your patent rights if you default on your loan.

For example, in 2017, Snapdeal, an Indian e-commerce company, mortgaged its patents on its online payment platform Freecharge, to HDFC Bank, to secure a loan of $47 million. The loan was used to fund Snapdeal's operations and expansion, and to compete with its rivals, such as Flipkart and Amazon. However, the loan also increased Snapdeal's debt and liabilities, and put its patent rights at stake if it failed to repay the loan.

Strengthening your resume: A patent can help you to strengthen your resume, as it showcases your skills, knowledge, and achievements. This can help you to enhance your career prospects and opportunities, and to impress your potential employers or collaborators. However, this also means that you have to keep updating and improving your skills and knowledge, and to be prepared for the challenges and expectations of your career or field.

For example, in 2018, Pranav Mistry, an Indian computer scientist and inventor, was appointed as the president and CEO of Samsung's STAR Labs, a research and development unit of the South Korean tech giant. Mistry is known for his inventions of various innovative technologies, such as the SixthSense wearable device, the Samsung Galaxy Gear smartwatch, and the Samsung Neon artificial humans. Mistry has filed and obtained several patents for his inventions, and has received numerous awards and recognition for his work. His patents have helped him to strengthen his resume and to advance his career in the tech industry.

Earning you promotions, praises and recognition: A patent can help you to earn promotions, praises and recognition, as it reflects your contribution and value to your organization or society. This can help you to boost your morale and motivation, and to increase your status and influence in your organization or society. However, this also means that you have to maintain and demonstrate your performance and productivity, and to be ready for the responsibilities and challenges of your role or position.

For example, in 2019, Ritu Karidhal and Minal Rohit, two Indian women scientists and engineers, were part of the team that led the Chandrayaan-2 mission, India's second lunar exploration mission. Karidhal and Rohit were responsible for the design and development of the mission's orbiter and lander, respectively, and they had filed and obtained several patents for their inventions related to the mission. Their patents have helped them to earn promotions, praises and recognition, both within their organization, the Indian Space Research Organization (ISRO), and outside, from the media, the public, and the government.

These are some of the indirect benefits of patenting your invention in India, but there may be other benefits as well, depending on your specific situation and goals.

Only Ground breaking and complex inventions get patent ?

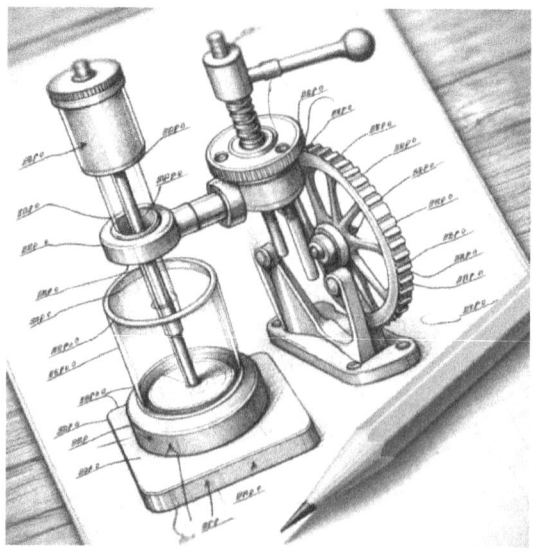

Most people misbelieve that, *Patents are given to only ground breaking (landmark) and complex invention that changes the world...*

Which is not true. In reality the patents are also **granted to incremental inventions** !!! Inventions that have novel solution to a technical problem, may that problem be small (but significant to form an inventive step and clear non obviousness test).

What that means is, most of the part of your solution may be already known to public (that is available in the market, patented or published in journals) but you might have come up with something (an inventive step) that is not an obvious solution to normal person skilled in that domain and solve a very small problem in existing solutions. In this such case the inventor still can win patent for his invention if other patentability criteria's are mate by his invention

Many inventors getting discouraged by seeing something similar to their invention in the market, published or known to public... what they fail to realize is they may still have novelty and inventive step in their invention although apparently it looks similar to things already known to public.

Don't get discouraged if you see things already in the market, published or known to public which are somewhat similar to your invention... You still may have something in your invention that can win patent.

This is beautifully explained in chapter number 2 "Idea incubation phase".

Many people misbelieve that patents are given to only ground-breaking (landmark) and complex inventions that change the world. They think that patents are reserved for inventions that are revolutionary, radical, or disruptive, such as the telephone, the airplane, or the internet. However, this is not true.
In reality, patents are also granted to incremental inventions. Incremental inventions are inventions that have novel solutions to technical problems, may that problem be small (but significant to form an inventive step and clear non-obviousness test).

Incremental inventions are inventions that improve, modify, or refine existing inventions, rather than creating new ones. Incremental inventions are inventions that are evolutionary, gradual, or incremental, rather than revolutionary, radical, or disruptive.

What that means is, most of the part of your solution may be already known to the public (that is available in the market, patented, or published in journals) but you might have come up with something (an inventive step) that is not an obvious solution to a normal person skilled in that domain and solve a very small problem in existing solutions. In this case, the inventor still can win a patent for his invention if other patentability criteria are met by his invention.

Many inventors get discouraged by seeing something similar to their invention in the market, published, or known to the public. What they fail to realize is that they may still have novelty and inventive step in their invention, although apparently it looks similar to things already known to the public.

Don't get discouraged if you see things already in the market, published, or known to the public that are somewhat similar to your invention. You still may have something in your invention that can win a patent.

To illustrate this point, here are some examples and case laws of incremental inventions that have been granted patents in India:

The patent for **a new and improved toothbrush by Colgate**: In 2006, Colgate, a US-based oral care company, filed a patent application in India for a new and improved toothbrush, which had a novel design and shape of the bristles, the head, and the handle. The patent claimed that the new toothbrush could provide better cleaning and comfort to the users, and could prevent tooth decay and gum diseases. The patent was granted in 2010, after overcoming the objections raised by the IPO, who initially rejected the patent application on the grounds of lack of novelty and inventive step. The IPO argued that the new toothbrush was not substantially different from the existing toothbrushes in the market, and that the claimed features were obvious to a person skilled in the art. However, Colgate submitted evidence and arguments to show that the new toothbrush had a novel and inventive combination of features, that were not disclosed or suggested by the prior art, and that provided a technical advantage and a surprising effect to the users. The IPO accepted Colgate's arguments and granted the patent to

Colgate.

The patent for a **new and improved mosquito repellent by Godrej**: In 2012, Godrej, an Indian consumer goods company, filed a patent application in India for a new and improved mosquito repellent, which had a novel composition and formulation of natural and synthetic ingredients. The patent claimed that the new mosquito repellent could provide better protection and safety to the users, and could repel mosquitoes more effectively and efficiently. The patent was granted in 2016, after overcoming the objections raised by the IPO, who initially rejected the patent application on the grounds of lack of novelty and inventive step. The IPO argued that the new mosquito repellent was not substantially different from the existing mosquito repellents in the market, and that the claimed features were obvious to a person skilled in the art. However, Godrej submitted evidence and arguments to show that the new mosquito repellent had a novel and inventive combination of ingredients, that were not disclosed or suggested by the prior art, and that provided a technical advantage and a surprising effect to the users. The IPO accepted Godrej's arguments and granted the patent to Godrej.

The patent for a **new and improved LED bulb by Philips**: In 2014, Philips, a Dutch electronics company, filed a patent application in India for a new and improved LED bulb, which had a novel design and structure of the LED chip, the heat sink, and the driver. The patent claimed that the new LED bulb could provide better performance and durability to the users, and could reduce the energy consumption and the heat generation of the bulb. The patent was granted in 2018, after overcoming the objections raised by the IPO, who initially rejected the patent application on the grounds of lack of novelty and inventive step. The IPO argued that the new LED bulb was not substantially different from the existing LED bulbs in the market, and that the claimed features were obvious to a person skilled in the art. However, Philips submitted evidence and arguments to show that the new LED bulb had a novel and inventive combination of features, that were not disclosed or suggested by the prior art, and that provided a technical advantage and a surprising effect to the users. The IPO accepted Philips' arguments and granted the patent to Philips.

These examples and case laws show that patents are not only given to ground-breaking and complex inventions that change the world, but also to incremental inventions that have novel solutions to technical problems, may that problem be small.

Therefore, if you have an invention that meets the criteria of patentability, such as novelty, inventive step, and industrial applicability, you should not hesitate to file a patent application in India, even if your invention is similar to things already known to the public. You may still have something in your invention that can win a patent.

What can be patented?

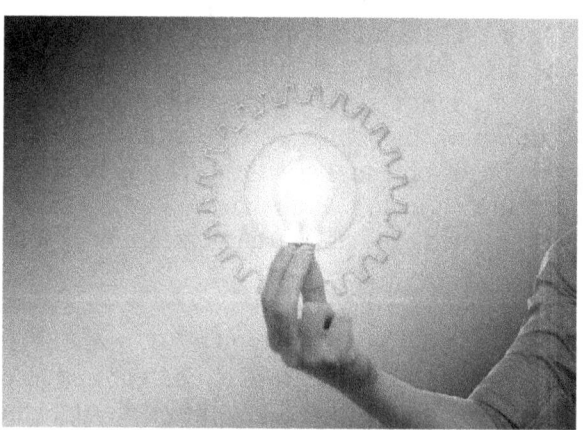

If you remember from the definition we have seen earlier, an invention relating either to a product or process that is new, involving inventive step and capable of industrial application can be patented.

Provided the invention is not falling under the categories of inventions that are non- patentable under section 3 and 4 of the Patent Act. (for details see section on inventions not patentable)

Here is how an **invention is defined** in patent act 1970:

Section 2(1)(j) "invention" means a new product or process involving an inventive step and capable of industrial application;

Section 2(1)(ja) "inventive step" means a feature of an invention that involves technical advance as compared to the existing knowledge or having economic significance or both and that makes the invention not obvious to a person skilled in the art

Section2(1)(ac) capable of industrial application", in relation to an invention, means that the invention is capable of being made or used in an industry;

Section 2(1)(l) "new invention" means any invention or technology which has not been anticipated by publication in any document or used in the country or elsewhere in the world before the date of filing of patent application with complete specification, i.e., the subject matter has not fallen in public domain or that it does not form part of the state of the art;

Patentable subject matter
Invention must
- relates to a Process or Product or both
- be new (Novel)
- involves an inventive step
- be Capable of industrial application
- not fall under Section 3 and 4

Patentability requirements of an invention

1. Newness or novelty
2. Inventive step or non-obviousness requirement
3. Capable of Industrial application
4. Enabling

What we can learn from it: If your innovative idea is a product or a process which has novelty, has an inventive step and is capable of industrial application then the invention said to be a patentable invention.

Now let's look at each patentability criteria one by one so that we can see if our innovative idea satisfies them and whether we should proceed with patent application.

Newness or novelty requirement:

Sections 2(1)(l) and 2(1)(j) of the Patents Act highlight the difference between a new invention and an invention. A 'new invention' is defined as:

"any invention or technology which has not been anticipated by publication in any document or used in the country or elsewhere in the world before the date of filing of patent application with complete specification, i.e., the subject matter has not fallen in public domain or that it does not form part of the state of the art".

An invention is said to be novel if all elements of a claim of the invention are not anticipated by a single prior art which is published, or used or known to public.

Refer chapter number 3. "working with patent agent or attorney" on patent drafting for understanding importance of claim and the role they play in patent.

Now let's talk about inventive step, also known as non obviousness test for your innovative idea.

An inventive step is said to be present in your invention when it has a technical advance as compared to the existing knowledge (that is state of the art of your field of invention) or it has economic significance or you invention has both such that it makes your invention non-obvious to a person skilled in the art.

So, we need to identify feature of our invention that is either **technically advance** or it is **economically significant** or both, when it is compared to state of the art or existing knowledge such that our invention becomes non-obvious to a person skilled in the art.

Technical advance means some feature of the invention is having advancement which is technical in nature as compared to the existing knowledge.

A person skilled in the art is a person who has average skills from your domain. For example if your invention is related to mechanical device the person skilled in the art would be from mechanical background. If there are multiple technologies used in the invention then a person skilled in the art is assumed to have all the knowledge (that is available and known to public) from the technologies involved. This is to assess the inventiveness of the invention.

The idea here is our invention should not be obvious to a person skilled in the art (that is an average person from a background of field of invention).

In other words, considering the state of the art (things already known to public) and assuming the person skilled in the art does not have any knowledge about our invention, if that person skilled in the art was asked to solve the problem (that our invention solves), then the our invention should not come as a natural suggestion by that person skilled in the art. Which ultimately means invention should not be obvious. This is in essence known as non obviousness test.

And one of the way to qualify for the non obviousness test of patentability is mentioning and proving to examiner that our invention is solving a the long standing problem in the industry. Pointing out that the problem existed for long time and there was a need to solve the problem, also mentioning existing prior arts and patent references who tried before but could not solve up to certain extent (stating problems with the prior arts in the background of the invention while drafting patent) and since the problem has not solved till now it ultimately means the solution to the problem that is our invention **was Not obvious**.

Now, this is not your job as an inventor to do all this, in fact this is responsibility of a patent agent or patent attorney working on your invention. an experienced patent professional would be asking you for required details and technicality of your invention and using such information while drafting patent application for your invention which gives a very good chance for your patent application to stand through examination stage till the grant of patent.

This is explained in detail in section "preparing patent application (patent drafting)" under chapter number 3. "working with patent agent or attorney"

Industrial application or utility

Section2(1)(ac) capable of industrial application", in relation to an invention, means that the invention is capable of being made or used in an industry;

Industrial application means invention is capable of being made or used in any kind of industry. This is also known as usefulness, a patented invention should be able to be produced on a large scale that is it could be created, used and repeated.

Now if you observe the word in definition is **Capable of** industrial application, which means it need not be mass produced right now, but has capability of industrial application in future. In general this patentability requirement of usefulness or industrial application is not much of a problem to prove.

Patentability criteria in India

To obtain a patent for your invention in India, you have to meet the following criteria of patentability, as per the Patents Act, 1970 and the Patents Rules, 2003:

- **Newness or novelty:** Your invention must be new or novel, meaning that it must not have been disclosed or anticipated by the prior art. The prior art refers to any information or knowledge that is available to the public before the date of filing or priority of your patent application, such as publications, patents, products, or public use. Your invention must have at least one feature or element that is different from the prior art, and that makes your invention unique and original.
- **Inventive step or non-obviousness requirement:** Your invention must have an inventive step or a non-obviousness requirement, meaning that it must not be obvious to a person skilled in the art. A person skilled in the art refers to a hypothetical person who has the ordinary level of skill and knowledge in the field of your invention, and who is aware of the prior art. Your invention must have a feature or element that is not obvious to such a person, and that involves a technical advancement or a problem-solving approach.
- **Capable of industrial application:** Your invention must be capable of industrial application, meaning that it must be useful and practical, and that it must be able to be made or used in any kind of industry. Industry refers to any physical or technical activity that produces goods or services, such as agriculture, manufacturing, or services.

Your invention must have a specific, substantial, and credible utility or purpose, and it must not be abstract, theoretical, or speculative.

In addition to these criteria of patentability, you also have to meet the requirement of **enabling disclosure**, meaning that you have to disclose your invention in a clear and complete manner in your patent application, and that you have to enable a person skilled in the art to make or use your invention without undue burden or experimentation. Your patent application must contain a description, claims, abstract, and drawings of your invention, and it must provide sufficient and relevant information and details about your invention, such as its technical field, background, objective, features, advantages, embodiments, examples, and best mode.

Inventions not patentable

What is **not** Patentable?

- o Inventions falling within the scope of Sec. (3) of Patents Act, 1970.
- o Inventions falling within the scope of Sec. (1) of Sub-sec. 20 of Atomic Energy Act, 1962-

The following are not inventions as per **Section 3** of patent act

(a) an invention which is frivolous or which claims anything obviously contrary to well established natural laws;

(b) an invention the primary or intended use or commercial exploitation of which could be contrary to public order or morality or which causes serious prejudice to human, animal or plant life or health or to the environment;

(c)   the mere discovery of a scientific principle or the formulation of an abstract theory or discovery of any living thing or non-living substance occurring in nature;

(d) the mere discovery of a new form of a known substance which does not result in the enhancement of the known efficacy of that substance or the mere discovery of any new property or new use for a known substance or of the mere use of a known process, machine or apparatus unless such known process results in a new product or employs at least one new reactant.

(e) a substance obtained by a mere admixture resulting only in the aggregation of the properties of the components thereof or a process for producing such substance;

(f) the mere arrangement or re-arrangement or duplication of known devices each functioning independently of one another in a known way;

(g)..(omitted)

(h) a method of agriculture or horticulture;

(i) any process for the medicinal, surgical, curative, prophylactic diagnostic, therapeutic or other treatment of human beings or any process for a similar treatment of animals to render them free of disease or to increase their economic value or that of their products.

(j) plants and animals in whole or any part thereof other than micro-organisms but including seeds, varieties and species and essentially biological processes for production or propagation of plants and animals;

(k) a mathematical or business method or a computer programme per se or algorithms;

(l) a literary, dramatic, musical or artistic work or any other aesthetic creation whatsoever including cinematographic works and television productions;

(m) a mere scheme or rule or method of performing mental act or method of playing game;

(n) a presentation of information;

(o) topography of integrated circuits;

(p) an invention which in effect, is traditional knowledge or which is an aggregation or duplication of known properties of traditionally known component or components.

And as per **Section 4** of patent act Inventions relating to atomic energy not patentable.

Section	Non-Patentable Inventions	Example 1	Example 2
3(a)	Invention contrary to natural laws	Perpetual motion machine	A machine that operates indefinitely without energy input
3(b)	Invention against public order or morality	Chemical substance for a highly addictive drug	Weapon designed to cause indiscriminate harm
3(c)	Discovery of natural substances	Discovery of a new mineral	Isolation of a new bacterium from soil without modification
3(d)	Known substance with no enhanced efficacy	New physical form of existing drug without improved efficacy	Crystal form of a chemical compound that doesn't increase potency
3(e)	Substance from mere admixture	Simple mixture of known fertilizers	Blend of known food preservatives without synergistic effect
3(f)	Arrangement of known devices	Flashlight combined with calculator	Physical combination of a phone and a camera
3(h)	Method of agriculture or horticulture	Traditional crop rotation method	Conventional method of planting seeds
3(i)	Treatment of humans or animals	Surgical procedure for common ailment	Therapy method for relieving joint pain
3(j)	Plants, animals, and biological processes for their making	New dog breed through conventional breeding	New plant variety created through standard cross-breeding
3(k)	Mathematical or business method, computer program	New mathematical formula for equations	Business method for online transactions
3(l)	Literary, dramatic, musical, artistic work	Novel or screenplay	Music composition

3(m)	Mental act, method of playing game	New strategy for playing chess	Method for solving a puzzle
3(n)	Presentation of information	Format for displaying weather data	New layout for a news website
3(o)	Topography of integrated circuits	Layout design of a semiconductor chip	Circuit design in consumer electronics
3(p)	Traditional knowledge, known properties aggregation	Herbal remedy using known medicinal plants	Traditional recipe for a food item
4	Inventions related to atomic energy	Process for enriching uranium	Design of a nuclear reactor component

Who can apply for patent in India?

An application for a Patent for an invention may be made by any of the following persons either alone or jointly with any other person:
- ☐ True and first inventor
- ☐ True and first inventor's assignee
- ☐ Legal representative of deceased true and first inventor or his/her assignee

According to Section 6 of the Patents Act, 1970, any person can apply for a patent in India, if he or she is the true and first inventor of an invention, or is an assignee or a legal representative of such person. An invention is defined as a new product or process involving an inventive step and capable of industrial application. An assignee is a person who has acquired the right to apply for a patent from the inventor by way of a valid assignment. A legal representative is a person who represents the estate of a deceased person who was entitled to apply for a patent before his or her death.

Some examples of who can apply for a patent in India are:

- A scientist who has invented a new vaccine for a disease can apply for a patent in India, as he or she is the true and first inventor of the invention.
- A company that has bought the patent rights of a new device from the inventor can apply for a patent in India, as it is the assignee of the inventor.
- A son or daughter of an inventor who has died before filing a patent application for a new method can apply for a patent in India, as he or she is the legal representative of the inventor.

2. Idea incubation phase

Idea Incubation Phase

- How to identify innovative ideas with potential to win patent
- How to get absolute clarity on your idea, being specific
- How to do a preliminary search for your innovative idea
- How to review the results you got from this preliminary search
- when to get encouraged and when to get discouraged for going ahead for patent filing based on results
- Creating Final Draft of working invention disclosure
- Mistakes to avoid in Idea incubation phase
- Action items, checklist, worksheet for Idea incubation phase that will help you to create your complete invention disclosure.

Link for video

"Everything begins with an idea."

– Earl Nightengale

This is probably the most important chapter of the book for you (the inventor) because if you remember when we were going through the steps and procedure for patent at idea incubation phase in your involvement as an inventor is 100% compared to patent professional (not involved yet) and patent office (not involved yet).

We are looking for a very specific outcome from this section:

The steps here are designed to take your innovative ideas from inception level, that is initial vague ideas about some solution to a problem to a comprehensive invention disclosure (that is ready to discuss with patent agent or attorney) which is the most important starting point the decides the future and fate of your innovative idea.

This is guideline helps you in moving from point A to point B

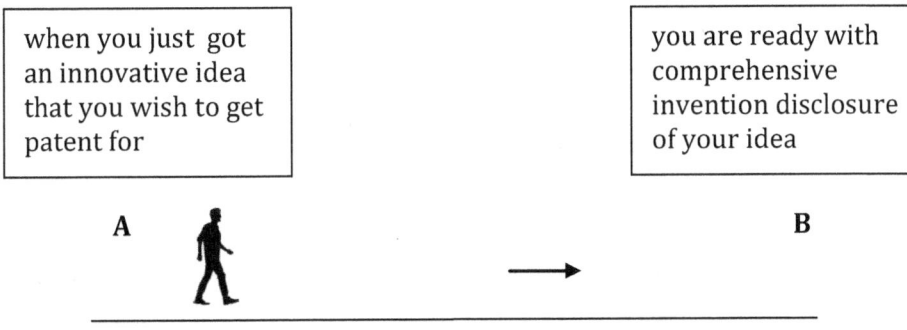

Point A is when you get an innovative idea, and you are thinking to yourself that probably this idea could win patent.

Point B is where, you are ready with comprehensive invention disclosure with along with the important information you came across while doing preliminary research about novelty and having closest possible prior arts already identified and included with comprehensive understanding about possible *Inventive step* of invention. hence creating a very informed starting point and invention disclosure that your patent agent / attorney can start working on it right away.

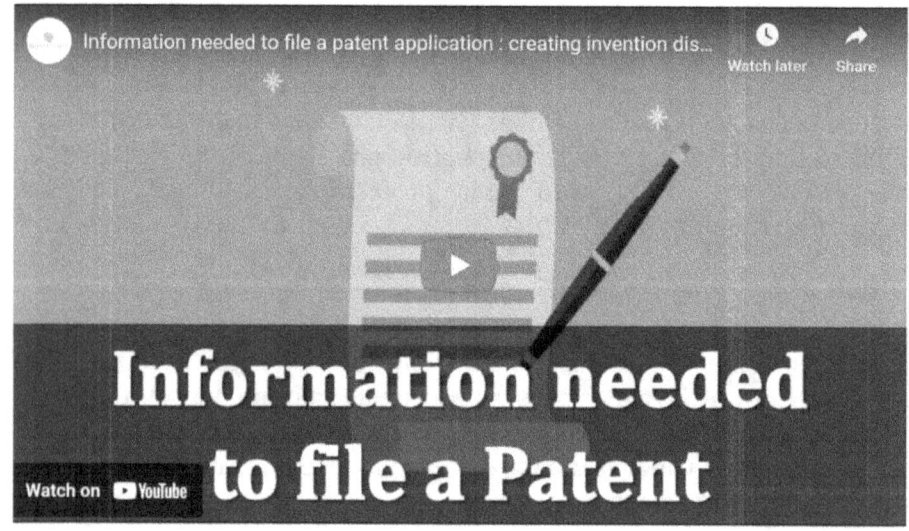

Link to video

Let's get started,

Get clarity on Idea

The way we get more and more clarity about our innovative ideas is when we start writing down things on paper or in a word processor document:

Start taking notes of details about the innovative idea, and get complete idea on a paper or a soft copy document, this is rough draft of your idea and by no means it need to be perfect or complete, just get started with this.

Action Items: Capture all details of idea

- o What is my innovative idea is about?
- o What problem it solve?
- o How does it solve the problem?
- o What are some advantages of my innovative idea?
- o Technical details about idea and how it function
- o Important elements of it
- o Block diagram or flow chart or any other relevant diagrams to explain the idea in better way.

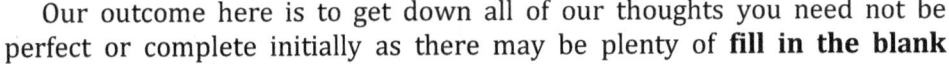

Our outcome here is to get down all of our thoughts you need not be perfect or complete initially as there may be plenty of **fill in the blank**

elements that you still don't have clarity upon that's pretty natural and we will be filling those elements as and when we proceed.

"we call it as a brain dump !!!"

brain-dump is a complete transfer of accessible knowledge about a particular subject from your brain to some other storage medium, such as paper or your computer's hard drive

In the next phase, try to come up with as many diagram or flowchart or whatever the convenient way of explaining your ideas and get more clarity on your innovative idea. again this would be **only rough sketches,** don't worry about the perfection here just get everything in front of you.

Preliminary search

Now, with the idea complete captured, or in some cases the outcome of research and development is completely capture as per actions items above, we are going to perform a small research, we call it as **preliminary search.**

There are two aspects of doing this research:

1. first aspect is try to find if somebody has already developed such an idea, and
2. second aspect is to get a brief idea and understanding about the level of awareness of the market (existing knowledge or state of the art) about your innovative idea.

Here we are trying to understand the **state of the art** or existing knowledge about related to our invention:

so, it is just a preliminary search performed by you (inventor) the objective is just to get the feel of the technology and state of the art (existing knowledge) about your invention, and if possible try to find the novel part and inventive step in our innovative idea (invention).

Now, this is by no means going to replace the comprehensive patentability search performed by a patent agent or attorney.

You may spend around 1 to 3 days to perform preliminary search.

Checklist for doing preliminary search

- o How many results we are getting that are really close to our innovative idea or talking something similar to our idea?
- o How many products or services are there already in the market that are similar to our invention
- o What is the extent of knowledge is already known to public in field of our invention, is there any uniqueness in our innovative idea?
- o How our invention is different or better than the prior art... or other products known to public
- o Do our idea have novelty? or some part of our invention that is not known to public?

Another important thing is to create and maintain list of keywords that we use to define our innovative idea. You will start with very few keywords, like your version of preferred terms you use for elements,

For example: you would be calling a computer processor as CPU (central procession unit) for our invention, however others may call it a image processor or information processing unit or signal processing system etc...depending on preference of words and language they use, and these all words might be used by different people at different places like articles, blogs, videos, patents, IEEE papers, books to necessarily explain exactly same thing !!!

so to be as comprehensive as possible with our preliminary research we need to build a list of keywords that we used to describe main elements of our innovative idea and its synonyms and other variations that you came across while doing research and reviewing results.

Let's say one of the element is a CCTV camera in our invention, then by finding synonyms for this elements and while doing research we came across different version of names for essentially same or similar device...

see the worksheet below, so updating the list of keywords and synonyms would be **ongoing process** and the list of keywords would keep getting mature and comprehensive as we progress.

List of keywords and synonyms found

Element 1   **Element 2**   **Element 3**

CCTV system
Surveillance system
Camera unit
Image capturing system
Video capturing unit
Live video recording
Video recorder
Video sensor
Image sensor
Etc...

Now, preliminary search becomes more and more accurate and shows more relevant results When we start using different combination of keywords from our list. If you able to search with fairly **accurate keyword combinations** related to your idea then chances are you will come across a lot of articles, blogs and sometimes there may be companies and products **very similar to your invention** will show up in the search results.

How to search

- ❑ when you have complete information about your invention in front of you; You can start performing search for finding closest possible prior arts
- ❑ start with basic keywords and then start adding different variations of keywords using the list of synonyms and different nomenclature that we have enlisted in previous section
- ❑ you can start with simple Google search, and slowly build the research on patent specific websites like Google patents, USPTO, European patent search, Indian patent search etc...
- ❑ so probability is you will come across some important prior arts for your innovative idea which are most readily searchable, and easily available on internet

Now, It is important **Not to get discouraged** here seeing a lot of stuff online that is similar to your innovative idea. Keep a good record of the results you feel are very closely related to our invention and create a folder to save these results. We call them closest possible prior arts. Find as many as possible and keep its record, we are going to review them at later stage and these are going to prove important in patent drafting / writing phase as well.

How to review results of preliminary search

If you remember the definition of a new invention from chapter 1,

Section 2(1)(l) "new invention" means any invention or technology which has not been anticipated by publication in any document or used in the country or elsewhere in the world before the date of filing of patent application with complete specification, i.e., the subject matter has not fallen in public domain or that it does not form part of the state of the art;

Now, let me clear it again; we are not replacing a patentability search which is done by patent agent or attorney here. Our only objective is to find the newness of the innovative idea.

While reviewing results we are comparing our invention and elements of our invention with the results found (that is prior arts, existing knowledge) and ideally **some aspects** of our invention should be new / novel which is not mentioned in prior art. It is important to know that

*"patents are not only given for ground breaking inventions, where as in reality patents are granted for **incremental inventions** too. That is incremental improvements in existing systems that are known to public."*

What we can understand from this (and what is really encouraging) is even if our innovative idea has some aspect that may be very small (yet significant to qualify for inventive step. See definition in chapter 1) you we can win patent for that invention. In other words, we might have 95% of elements of our invention which are known to public and in existing knowledge But even if we have 5% of our invention that is some small part of our invention which is novel, which is non-obvious to a person skilled in the art and which has industrial application then our invention would be patentable !!!

And this is a **great news**... isn't it !!!

What we can learn from this is do not get discouraged seeing thousands of or even lacks of results in your search talking something similar to our invention, our invention still might have some inventive step in it which could win patent. when we are reviewing results and closest possible prior arts, look for following things and take a note of it:

find the ways in which your invention is different or rather better in getting intended results or solving existing problem. maybe you have some of points in your inventions as below:
- some aspect of it may be technically advanced or economically significant or both
- Your way to solve the problem is more energy efficient
- your compound, medicine may be having more efficacy
- your software or application is doing some advance things to solve a problem than existing solutions

---

When we are reviewing results

- ❑ find out how our invention is different or improved in one or the other aspects when we compare it with the prior art
- ❑ Take specific notes of things where our innovative idea solve some problem in existing prior art or the state of the art
- ❑ Particularly look for elements of our invention which are different and which are improved compared to the prior arts found

Take a good note of differences in front of each result after the review so that you can discuss it with patent agent / attorney at appropriate stage.

The improvement may seemingly small but it still can win patent if it is novel, non obvious (that is having inventive step) and is having industrial application.

It is important to understand **not to get discouraged** while seeing hundreds and thousands of similar patents or articles or blog post talking similar thing like your innovative idea because, there is every chance that you are innovative idea might have at least incremental invention that we could discover at detailed discussion and review with a patent agent /attorney. And a good patent application writing specifically pointing out **novel and non-obvious aspects** of the invention while writing claims would eventually will be rewarded with patent.

Now, you are not expected to do patentability analysis of invention on your own in fact this is done by experienced patent agents and attorneys after performing extensive research for 5 to 7 days, we are not expecting such judgment from you (the inventor).

Instead, we want to address an important problem here that inventor gets discouraged by seeing a lot of results, products, patent and articles in his area and abandons the follow-up or research and development effort although his innovative idea (invention) might be patentable !!!

So, **do not get discouraged** and take next step.

Having said that, there is other side to it as well. When you see that there are many results in the search that talk exactly same like your invention and in fact there are products and services about it being used by public and there is nothing new or improved in your invention when compared to existing knowledge, that is 100% knock out by many prior arts / existing knowledge...

Then probably yes, you may get discouraged and stop following up with that innovative idea. I would still say get opinion from patent professional before you conclude on this too.

At the end of this preliminary search what we have is :

✓ a detailed description of invention where every aspect of it is

completely captured
- ✓ Diagrams, flowcharts and illustrations if applicable
- ✓ comprehensive list of keywords, synonyms and search terms
- ✓ all results of preliminary search reviewed
- ✓ list of closest possible prior arts
- ✓ differences and problems with prior arts that our invention is solving
- ✓ some aspect of our invention that are novel and non-obvious

having all this information in front of us, now we are in position to create most **comprehensive invention disclosure** also called working disclosure of the invention.

Below are list of questions to which we need to find answers to be able to create a complete invention disclosure

Invention disclosure

Your invention disclosure needs to answer these questions (if not all of them, as many as possible):

- ❑ How you have come up with this innovative idea?
- ❑ What is your invention about?
- ❑ What problem your invention is solving?
- ❑ What are the advantages of your invention?
- ❑ What are important elements or components of your invention?
- ❑ Draw a block diagram or device or flowchart or sketch that explains your invention in better way
- ❑ What products or services that are already in the market which are similar to your invention
- ❑ How your invention is different or improved or efficient than already existing knowledge
- ❑ What components are unique and non-obvious to a person skilled in the art
- ❑ What is the inventive step in your invention that is either technical advanced or economic significance or both
- ❑ Who are the main competitors working in the same field of my

innovative idea and what are their products or services
- ❏ Does any publication, articles, news, blog, PDF, book, video or patents completely disclosure your invention
- ❏ What part of your invention is crucially important for commercialization
- ❏ How your invention is better than the prior arts and existing knowledge
- ❏ what are the limitations of existing patents or prior art and how your invention is providing solution to those problems
- ❏ can you explain my invention in to granular details such that the disclosure becomes enabling, that is a person skilled in the art should be able to practice their invention without doing additional research just by reading my disclosure of invention.
- ❏ include outcome of experiments or results in table formats, graphs or any charts related to your innovative idea (if applicable)
- ❏ can you mention important elements to be included in claims

although these questions are too many and you probably don't need to answer all of them however you could easily come up with answers to all of them in much better way now... because you have done preliminary search

The collection of information which answers questions above creates a **comprehensive invention disclosure**.

You will have a very important information collected in the folder which would include:

1. Final version of invention disclosure
2. downloaded and reviewed prior art documents
3. your review notes about prior arts mentioning how our invention is different or improved
4. Informed and detailed answers to invention disclosure form
5. your personal notes and opinion about what you think is really novel as per your research and where are **commercial important aspects** of this invention
6. And if possible guideline on **where to focus** when writing and drafting the patent application

Now, when you talk to your patent agent or attorney you know inside out what exactly that you are looking to protect and most important of all you will start with **meaningful discussions** with your patent attorney from the first call itself, simply because the kind of clarity that you have about your invention and the current state of the art related to the field of invention.

How this will save time and costs

Now having done such an important work on your innovative idea before even contacting to patent agent or attorney (that is following all steps in Idea incubation phase), this will save a lot of efforts, time and ultimately costs when you are moving ahead with patent filing for invention. Particularly this helps in:

- eliminating a lot of rework / additional research
- to and fro communications and
- delays in communication from your end because you are not prepared with required information

This will drastically reduced it to and fro communications which will really help in reducing the **time and costs to file the patent application** as there would be no rework and crystal clear expectations are set from the word go.

And most important of all is your patent agent / attorney going to **love working with you** because you probably are one of the most informed client he has came across, and he need not educate you while working with you, most of patent agents/attorneys would be delighted by the efforts you took to understand the novel and non-obvious part of your invention and coming up with really good invention disclosure and may provide you with discounts in the professional fees up to certain extent.

Of course patent agent /attorneys will do their patentability search, they will come up with their own patentability search report and then share it with you and you would be reviewing it with them. but what you have done for now (in this idea incubation phase) really going to help you in a great deal in getting very close to our **main outcome**. (refer page no. 5 of introduction) that is "getting the maximum protection for your invention in shortest possible time and at lowest possible cost."

Mistakes to avoid in idea incubation phase

Mistake 1: Wasting your valuable time, efforts and money on Innovative ideas that are already known to public.

Taking innovative idea to patent attorney **too early** and directly without doing much of background check. in this case the problem would be wasting time efforts and money on innovative ideas which you yourself would have known prior to giving to patent attorney that the idea is not yet completely developed, or is not at all patentable because this innovative idea is known to public already and was easily discoverable upon doing little bit of research by inventor himself.

Mistake 2: Waiting too long to perfect innovative idea

Second mistake would be analysis paralysis that is waiting for too long to take your innovative ideas to patent agent or attorney. this is the mistake which is initiated by the belief that your inventions should have something groundbreaking new thing to be able to win patent.

Too early and too late both are dangerous when it comes to filing patent application for the invention. If you are too early, you may be in a ideation stage and research and development still going on, so complete description of invention to get patent might not yet be available with you. hence you might not be protecting the invention with appropriately scope.

And if you are too late, chances are you would lose the priority or even invention since competitors may come up with same patent application before you file one.

Other such mistakes to avoid are

- Vague Descriptions: Avoid being too vague or general in describing your invention. Be specific about its features, functions, and components.
- Overlooking Prior Art Search: Failing to conduct a comprehensive prior art search to ensure your invention is novel and non-obvious.

- Ignoring Alternative Embodiments: Not considering and describing alternative versions or embodiments of the invention.
- Neglecting Drawings and Diagrams: Omitting detailed drawings or diagrams that can clarify and support the textual description.
- Lack of Problem and Solution Explanation: Not clearly defining the problem your invention solves or how it improves upon existing solutions.
- Missing Detailed Implementation: Forgetting to include detailed implementation details like materials, dimensions, or manufacturing processes.
- Failure to Describe All Elements: Not describing every element of the invention and how these elements interact.

3. Working with a patent agent or attorney

Save time, costs while working with a patent agent or attorney:

- Non disclosure Agreement
- How the Idea incubation phase, if done correctly is really helpful here
- Effective first call or email with a patent agent or attorney firm
- how to proactively speed up the patenting process
- how to be ready with expected information at appropriate stages
- Opinion about patentability
- Making decision to go ahead with patent filing based on results
- Preparing Patent application (Patent drafting)
- Important rules for patent claims, detailed description, drawings, references, title, Abstract etc.
- Covering all possible embodiments
- How to ensure that the patent application is written to provide **broadest possible protection** for your innovative idea

Do I really need patent agent or patent attorney ?

Link for video

We will address this question upfront,

The reason behind this question is obvious, you are trying to figure out whether it is worth going for such an expense to go with patent agent / attorney to file a patent application. Or can I just take the forms that are provided, fill in the details and submit it to patent office? This is basic question that every inventor has when he decides to go ahead for filing patent for his invention.

to answer this question in unbiased way let's take one step back and try to understand who exactly patent agent is…

as you already might be knowing patent is a techno-legal document, as an inventor you are the best person to who understands the invention technically but when it comes to legal as it is a **patent law** (the patent act) you probably won't have that kind of experience or that wisdom to write a patent application considering the legal side of patent.

so let's search few patents from your domain area which is the area of your invention, go on Google patents and try to come up with some granted patents from your domain.

for example you may have mechanical device or idea for software application or E-commerce website to patent. Just type in relevant search keywords and review some results. Look at the **construction of patent,** have a look at how description is written, how the diagrams are marked and labeled, how detailed the description is written. and then most important part of patent , claims. Observe the language of claims. Structure and order of claim, broader scope claims and narrow claims etc...

You will quickly realize that this is way different than the normal thesis or project report or any technical document you have seen. There is a reason behind.

Patent documents are one of the **most complex documents** involve certain degree of difficulty in creating while considering technical side as well as legal side. After all it is a Law, and like any other law, there are sections, act, rules, general guidelines, case laws, historical wisdom (wisdom from cases and their results) are involved.

So there are way too many aspects, rules, sections and general practices followed by experienced patent practitioners while writing patent application for your invention which is almost impossible to match by a first time inventors.

And interesting thing to know is, patent office knows that inventors might need help in creating patent application so patent agents and patent attorney are authorized by government to practice before government patent office for patent procedures that is patent prosecution and litigations.

So, registered patent agents and attorneys are made available by government itself. there is an exam for registered patent agents which an extensive very difficult level exam. And they are established by government of India itself to help inventors in patent procedures.

The main advantage here is patent agents and attorneys are also science graduates, like electronics, computer, chemical engineers or pharmaceutical or biotech graduates, so they are equally qualified to understand the technical side of invention as well.

An experienced patent professional stand in your (inventors) shoes and understand invention from your point of view. and he leverage his wisdom of writing patent application as he would have seen hundreds of if not thousands of patents in his career.

Can I do it myself without patent professional ?

It is possible. You can file the patent application without help from patent professional, in that case it is advisable that you should at least get your patent application reviewed by an experienced patent agent or attorney before filing into the patent office.

because writing a good patent application involves **so much more** than a first timer can accommodate into his / her writing, even trained patent professional require at least 3 to 5 years of experience to be able to write reasonably good it in the application. Hence it is worth giving a second thought to it, if you have decided to do it yourself.

A patent application not written properly, could prove a **costly mistake** in future as it will not protect your invention as you expected it to do and it will probably not worth the time and effort you put to get the invention protected.

There are rules about so many things while writing patent application:
- ✓ Rules about writing title of image
- ✓ rules for writing abstract
- ✓ how claims should be written
- ✓ how detailed description is to be written
- ✓ rules for drawings
- ✓ rules for numbering the drawings
- ✓ rules for pages

it is very likely that the first time inventor or do-it-yourself writer of patent application would be making some **obvious mistakes** that could prove costly in the longer term, and if your invention is worth patenting it probably is worth having a patent agent or attorney.

Explanation about the question "Can I draft and file patent application on my own ? without patent agent or attorney?"

The answer is: Yes, you can, but it is not advisable. Doing it yourself without patent professional may seem tempting, as it may save you some money and time, but **it may also cost you more money and time, and even your patent rights, in the long run**.

Here are some of the reasons why you should not do it yourself without patent professional, and why you should hire a patent professional to help you with your patent process:

Writing a good patent application with broadest possible scope:

Writing a good patent application is not an easy task, as it requires a lot of skill and knowledge, not only in the technical field of the invention, but also in the legal field of the patent law. Writing a good patent application also requires a lot of strategy and creativity, as it involves defining the scope and validity of your patent rights, and anticipating and avoiding the possible objections and rejections from the patent office or the competitors.

A patent professional can help you write a good patent application, by using his or her qualification and expertise, and by following the format and requirements of the patent office. A patent professional can also help you write a patent application with the broadest possible scope, by drafting the claims, which are the statements that define the essential features and boundaries of your invention, and by using the appropriate language, terms, and expressions, that can cover the variations and modifications of your invention, without infringing the prior art.

A patent professional can also help you write a patent application with the broadest possible scope, by conducting a prior art search, which is a search of the existing information or knowledge that is relevant to your invention, such as publications, patents, products, or public use, and by distinguishing and differentiating your invention from the prior art, and by showing the novelty and inventive step of your invention.

For example, in 2017, the Delhi High Court upheld the validity of a patent for a new and improved hair dye, on the grounds that it was written by a patent professional with the broadest possible scope. The patent was granted to L'Oreal, a French cosmetics company, in 2008, for a new and improved hair dye, which had a novel composition and formulation of natural and synthetic ingredients. The patent was challenged by Godrej, an Indian consumer goods company, in 2010, on the grounds that it lacked novelty and inventive step, as it was anticipated by the prior art. The prior art was a patent application filed by Godrej in 2005, for a similar hair dye, which had a similar composition and formulation of natural and synthetic ingredients. The Delhi High Court held that L'Oreal's patent was valid, as it was written by a patent professional with the broadest possible scope, and as it had claims that covered the variations and modifications of the composition and formulation of the hair dye, without infringing the prior art. The Delhi High Court also held that L'Oreal's patent was valid, as it was written by a patent professional with the broadest possible scope, and as it had a prior art search, which showed the novelty and inventive step of the hair dye, and which distinguished and differentiated the hair dye from the prior art.

Prosecuting and defending the patent till grant

Prosecuting and defending the patent till grant is not a simple process, as it involves a lot of communication and negotiation with the patent office and the competitors, and a lot of documentation and evidence to support and prove your patent rights. Prosecuting and defending the patent till grant also involves a lot of challenges and risks, such as objections, rejections, oppositions, or revocations, that can affect the scope and validity of your patent rights.

A patent professional can help you prosecute and defend your patent till grant, by using his or her qualification and expertise, and by following the rules and procedures of the patent office. A patent professional can also help you prosecute and defend your patent till grant, **by responding to the objections, rejections, oppositions, or revocations, that may arise from the patent office** or the competitors, and by providing the arguments and evidence to overcome and counter them, and by showing the novelty, inventive step, and industrial applicability of your invention.

For example, in 2016, the Supreme Court of India upheld the grant of a patent for a new and improved vaccine for hepatitis B, on the grounds that it was prosecuted and defended by a patent professional till grant. The patent was granted to Bharat Biotech, an Indian biotechnology company, in 2006, for a new and improved vaccine for hepatitis B, which had a novel strain of the virus, and which had a higher efficacy and safety than the existing vaccines. The patent was opposed by Panacea Biotech, another Indian biotechnology company, in 2007, on the grounds that it lacked novelty and inventive step, as it was anticipated by the prior art. The prior art was a patent granted to Pasteur Institute, a French research institute, in 1990, for a vaccine for hepatitis B, which had a similar strain of the virus, and which had a similar efficacy and safety as the existing vaccines. The Supreme Court of India held that Bharat Biotech's patent was valid, as it was prosecuted and defended by a patent professional till grant, and as it had responded to the opposition from Panacea Biotech, and provided the arguments and evidence to overcome and counter it, and showed the novelty and inventive step of the vaccine, and distinguished and differentiated the vaccine from the prior art.

Common mistake if you are do it yourself

Some common mistakes done by inventors while filing patent application on their own are:

- ☐ The disclosure of invention is not sufficient enough and not enabling
- ☐ Claims are not supported in description of the invention
- ☐ Claims are not protecting the actual inventions properly
- ☐ The inventive step is not properly claimed
- ☐ The claims written are too limiting and lack the proper legal terms to be able to have border scope
- ☐ All possible variations and embodiments are not mentioned
- ☐ Best mode of practicing invention is not disclosed

And this list by no means complete, and many other type of mistakes that can raise a lot of **objections in the proceeding** of getting patent for your invention.

Having said that It has been observed that some inventors have written their patent application with remarkable quality and understanding of legal aspect of writing that it is hard to believe it is not written by an experienced patent attorney but by an inventor. However such cases are **very rare** and most often than not, inventors understand the technology part really well and but lack the understanding of legal aspects when writing patent application especially writing claims for the invention.

Mistakes of self-writing patent applications (DIY)

Writing a patent application on your own and filing it without help of a patent professional can be a risky and challenging task, as it involves a lot of technical and legal aspects, and a lot of formalities and procedures, that require a high level of skill and knowledge.

If you are not familiar with the patent law and practice in India, you may make some common and costly mistakes, that can affect the scope and validity of your patent rights, and that can delay or deny the grant of your patent.

Here are some of the mistakes that can happen if you are writing patent application on your own and filing it without help of a patent professional, and how to avoid them:

Mistakes in writing patent application: Writing a patent application is not a simple or straightforward task, as it requires a clear and complete description of your invention, and a precise and accurate definition of your claims, which are the statements that define the essential features and boundaries of your invention. If you are writing patent application on your own, you may make some mistakes in writing patent application, such as:

Writing a patent application that is too broad or too narrow: If you write a patent application that is too broad, you may claim more than what you have invented, and you may infringe the prior art, which is any information or knowledge that is available to the public before the date of filing or priority of your patent application, such as publications, patents, products, or public use.

If you write a patent application that is too narrow, you may claim less than what you have invented, and you may limit the scope and protection of your patent rights, and you may allow others to copy or modify your invention without your permission.

To avoid this mistake, you should write a patent application that is balanced and reasonable, and that covers the variations and modifications of your invention, without infringing the prior art.

Writing a patent application that is unclear or inconsistent: If you write a patent application that is unclear or inconsistent, you may create confusion or ambiguity in the interpretation or understanding of your invention, and you may face difficulties or objections in the examination or prosecution of your patent application.

To avoid this mistake, you should write a patent application that is clear and consistent, and that uses simple and precise language, and that follows the format and requirements of the patent office. You should also use drawings, diagrams, or sketches, to explain the working of your invention in a better way with visual illustrations.

Writing a patent application that is incomplete or inaccurate: If you write a patent application that is incomplete or inaccurate, you may omit or misrepresent some important information or details about your invention, and you may jeopardize the novelty and inventive step of your invention, which are the criteria of patentability, that require your invention to be new and non-obvious.

To avoid this mistake, you should write a patent application that is complete and accurate, and that provides sufficient and relevant information and details about your invention, such as its technical field, background, objective, features, advantages, embodiments, examples, and best mode. You should also disclose all the relevant prior art, and distinguish and differentiate your invention from the prior art.

Mistakes in filing patent application: Filing a patent application is not a simple or straightforward process, as it involves a lot of formalities and procedures, and a lot of communication and negotiation with the patent office and the competitors, and a lot of documentation and evidence to support and prove your patent rights. If you are filing patent application on your own, you may make some mistakes in filing patent application, such as:

Filing a patent application that is late or invalid: If you file a patent application that is late or invalid, you may lose the priority or the validity of your patent application, and you may lose your right to the invention over others.

To avoid this mistake, you should file a patent application as soon as possible, after you have a clear and complete idea of your invention, and after you have done some preliminary research and analysis on your own. You should file a patent application as soon as possible, to secure your priority date, which is the date on which you first file a patent application for your invention, and which determines your right to the invention over others.

You should also file a patent application as soon as possible, to prevent others from disclosing or using your invention, which can affect the novelty and inventive step of your invention.

You should also file a patent application that is valid, by complying with the formal and procedural requirements of the patent office, such as the language, format, fees, and timelines.

Filing a patent application that is incomplete or inaccurate: If you file a patent application that is incomplete or inaccurate, you may face difficulties or objections in the examination or prosecution of your patent application, and you may delay or deny the grant of your patent. To avoid this mistake, you should file a patent application that is complete and accurate, by providing all the necessary and correct information and documents, such as the description, claims, abstract, drawings, and forms, and by following the rules and procedures of the patent office. You should also file a patent application that is consistent with your invention, and that matches with your patent specification and claims.

Mistakes in responding to FER First examination report, hearing and communication with patent office: Responding to FER, hearing and communication with patent office is not a simple or straightforward task, as it requires a lot of skill and knowledge, not only in the technical field of the invention, **but also in the legal field of the patent law**.

If you are responding to FER, hearing and communication with patent office on your own, you may make some mistakes which can result in loss of patent rights and refusal of patent.

Writing patent application is a specialized skill

Link for video

Writing patent application requires fair understanding and experience in

☐ Patent law and patent office rules and regulations
☐ Case laws affecting the interpretation of patent law
☐ Technical skills of subject matter of the invention

As an inventor you can be a leading expert in your field of invention that is technical side of it that's your strength but where you may face challenge is legal side of it. Without (patent attorney or patent agent) chances are your patent application would be **just a technical description of the invention** and may fail for its sole purpose of "protecting your invention with broadest possible scope" refer our outcome expected from patent in introduction.

When you (inventor) work with right patent attorney (agent), it becomes a combination of your technical expertise + patent attorneys legal expertise and this can result into a very strong patent that adequately protects every aspect of your invention.

Advantages of going with patent agent or attorney

1. Patent agent and attorney would know how to write patent application and claims to have the **broadest possible protection** for your invention such that your competitors should not be able to copy your invention or just walk around your invention by changing some things and not infringing on your patent.

2. Writing a patent application itself has extensive laws, rules and procedures applicable, and number of things to consider, you would be surprised to know, there are rules related to margins of the page, rules for writing the title, abstract, claims, diagrams, detailed description, enabling etc...

3. The entire process of inception of idea to granted patent and beyond becomes a smooth experience for you when you have experienced patent agent / attorney guiding you at every stage...

you don't need to worry what kind of **forms** to use or **fees** to be paid, what kind of **notice** is there or what do you mean by **objections** raised, how to respond to objections etc…

all these kind of things are already taken care by patent agent or attorney and not to forget the **importance of dates** and subsequent steps you should be considering for entire procedure.

so patent attorney takes care of reminding you for every date and appropriate steps to be taken with right information.

So, these 3 things makes this investment in going for patent agent or attorney look pretty small if you are considering in the longer term that is the life of your invention and if at all you win the patent get 20 years from the filing date that you are going to enjoy monopoly on it.

ultimately I think it all depends on **level of seriousness** that you have with your invention if you are casual you can just try it out just submit whatever you think is appropriate and let see what happens with the response from patent office but if you are serious with your invention and don't want to lose its entire Novelty or **don't want to lose upon the opportunity** to take it to the next level then you should consider hiring a patent agent or attorney. It is well worth the investment.

On the other hand you can try writing and filing patent application on your own but as explained above it is almost impossible to match the level of well drafted patent application by an expert patent professional, and more often than not you will end up losing on the opportunity to protect your invention adequately and making significant money with it.

that's why patent agents and patent attorneys are there to help and they improve your chances to getting patent granted for your invention.

The responsibilities of patent agent / attorney

☐ Representing clients in all matters and procedures relating to patent law and practice

- Preparing application for patent
- Providing advice during patent application process
- Helps in drafting strong claims for your invention to be able to protect it in fullest possible extent
- prosecuting patent applications

By executing power of attorney, you (inventor) can appoint a patent attorney or agent to represent you for patent proceedings at Indian patent office.

We will discuss:
- some of the advantages of hiring a patent attorney or a patent agent for your invention,
- how the cost of this investment is justified in the form of a strong patent application,
- ensuring the patent will pass through examination phase till grant and
- beyond grant ensuring it could be enforced and commercialized so that to achieve a good ROI.

We will also illustrate these points with three real life examples and real case laws proving by analysis the cost of hiring patent agent or attorney is justified.

There are many advantages of hiring a patent attorney or a patent agent for your invention, such as:

Expertise, qualification and experience in Patents: Patent attorneys or patent agents offer important expertise to their clients. They understand both the legal and technical aspects of obtaining a patent. They have the qualification and experience to assist the inventor in preparing and filing the patent application, and in prosecuting and defending the patent against challenges or infringements. They are well-versed in the patent law and practice in India, and can guide the inventor through the complex maze of rules and regulations. They can also conduct thorough research and analysis to ensure the invention is novel and non-obvious, which are the criteria of patentability, and to distinguish and differentiate the invention from the prior art, which is any information or knowledge that is available to the public before the date of filing or priority of the patent application, such as publications, patents, products, or public use.

Maximize the protection of invention: Patent attorneys or patent agents can help the inventor to maximize the protection of their invention. They can help the inventor to write a strong patent application, that covers the variations and modifications of the invention, without infringing the prior art. They can also help the inventor to draft the claims, which are the statements that define the essential features and boundaries of the invention, and to use the appropriate language, terms, and expressions, that can cover the broadest possible scope of the invention, without being vague or ambiguous. They can also help the inventor to respond to the objections, rejections, oppositions, or revocations, that may arise from the patent office or the competitors, and to provide the arguments and evidence to overcome and counter them, and to show the novelty, inventive step, and industrial applicability of the invention.

Commercialization: Patent attorneys or patent agents can help the inventor to commercialize their invention. They can help the inventor to identify and evaluate the potential market and demand for the invention, and to devise a suitable business strategy and plan. They can also help the inventor to license, assign, or sell their patent rights to others, and to negotiate the terms and conditions of the agreement. They can also help the inventor to enforce their patent rights against any infringers, and to seek appropriate remedies, such as injunctions, damages, or royalties.

How the Cost of Hiring a Patent Attorney /Agent is justified

Hiring a patent attorney or a patent agent for your invention can have a decent cost to it. However, the cost of hiring a patent attorney or a patent agent can be justified in the long run, as they can provide you with **a strong patent** application, that can ensure the <u>patent will pass through examination phase till grant and beyond grant ensuring it could be enforced and commercialized so that to achieve a good ROI.</u>

Some of the ways how the cost of hiring a patent attorney or a patent agent is justified are:

- **Saving time and money:** Hiring a patent attorney or a patent agent can save you time and money in the patent process, as they can handle the formalities and procedures efficiently and effectively, and avoid any delays or errors that could jeopardize your patent rights. They can also save you time and money in the patent litigation, as they can represent you in the court or before the patent office, and provide you with the best possible outcome.

- **Securing priority and validity:** Hiring a patent attorney or a patent agent can secure your priority and validity of your patent application, as they can file your patent application as soon as possible, after you have a clear and complete idea of your invention, and after you have done some preliminary research and analysis on your own. They can also file your patent application that is valid, by complying with the formal and procedural requirements of the patent office, such as the language, format, fees, and timelines.

- **Preventing disclosure and infringement:** Hiring a patent attorney or a patent agent can prevent disclosure and infringement of your invention, as they can advise you on the confidentiality and secrecy of your invention, and the implications of disclosing or using your invention before filing the patent application. They can also help you to enforce your patent rights against any infringers, and to seek appropriate remedies, such as injunctions, damages, or royalties.

To illustrate the advantages of hiring a patent attorney or a patent agent for your invention, and how the cost of this investment is justified, we will discuss a real life examples proving by analysis the cost of hiring patent agent or attorney is justified.

Example 1: Cipla Ltd. vs. Hoffmann-La Roche Ltd. & Anr.

This is a case involving a pharmaceutical patent, where the Delhi High Court upheld the validity of a patent for a new and improved hair dye, on the grounds that it was written by a patent professional with the broadest possible scope. The patent was granted to L'Oreal, a French cosmetics company, in 2008, for a new and improved hair dye, which had a novel composition and formulation of natural and synthetic ingredients. The patent was challenged by Godrej, an Indian consumer goods company, in 2010, on the grounds that it lacked novelty and inventive step, as it was anticipated by the prior art. The prior art was a patent application filed by Godrej in 2005, for a similar hair dye, which had a similar composition and formulation of natural and synthetic ingredients.

The Delhi High Court held that L'Oreal's patent was valid, as it was written by a patent professional with the broadest possible scope, and as it had claims that covered the variations and modifications of the composition and formulation of the hair dye, without infringing the prior art. The Delhi High Court also held that L'Oreal's patent was valid, as it was written by a patent professional with the broadest possible scope, and as it had a prior art search, which showed the novelty and inventive step of the hair dye, and which distinguished and differentiated the hair dye from the prior art.

The return on investment (ROI) of getting a patent in India

for an invention depends on various factors, such as the market potential, the competitive advantage, the legal protection, and the social impact of the invention. A patent can provide a positive ROI for an inventor if it generates more income than the cost of obtaining and maintaining the patent, and if it prevents others from copying or exploiting the invention without permission. Here are some real-life case laws from India that illustrate the ROI of getting a patent for an invention:

Case 1: The Bajaj Auto case: In this case, Bajaj Auto, an Indian automobile company, applied for a patent for a two-wheeler vehicle with a digital twin spark ignition (DTS-i) technology. This technology improved the fuel efficiency and performance of the vehicle, and gave Bajaj Auto a competitive edge in the market. The patent was opposed by TVS Motor, another Indian automobile company, who claimed that they had already developed a similar technology called controlled combustion variable timing intelligent (CC-VTi) and that Bajaj Auto had infringed their patent. The case went to the Madras High Court, which ruled in favor of Bajaj Auto and granted them an interim injunction against TVS Motor. The court held that Bajaj Auto had a valid patent for their DTS-i technology and that TVS Motor had failed to prove that their CC-VTi technology was different from Bajaj Auto's DTS-i technology. **Bajaj Auto won the case and secured their exclusive right to use their DTS-i technology, which gave them a competitive edge in the market**.

The cost of hiring a patent agent or attorney for drafting, novelty search, response to FER, and hearing would have been much lower than the potential loss of revenue and reputation from the patent infringement.

Case 2: The Roche case. In this case, Roche, a Swiss pharmaceutical company, applied for a patent for a hepatitis C drug called Pegasys in India. This drug was a breakthrough in the treatment of hepatitis C, a chronic and life-threatening disease that affects millions of people in India. The patent was challenged by Sankalp Rehabilitation Trust, an Indian non-governmental organization, who claimed that the patent was invalid and that it prevented access to affordable treatment for hepatitis C patients in India. The case went to the Intellectual Property Appellate Board (IPAB), which upheld the validity of Roche's patent and rejected the challenge by Sankalp. The IPAB held that Roche's patent met the criteria of novelty, inventive step, and industrial applicability, and that it did not violate the public interest or the right to health. Roche retained the patent and the exclusive right to market Pegasys in India, which was a lucrative market for hepatitis C treatment.

The cost of hiring a patent agent or attorney for drafting, novelty search, response to FER, and hearing would have been much lower than the potential income from the patent, which was estimated to be around **300 million USD per year.**

Case 3: The Ericsson case. In this case, Ericsson, a Swedish telecommunications company, sued several Indian mobile phone manufacturers, such as Micromax, Intex, Lava, and Xiaomi, for infringing its standard essential patents (SEPs) relating to 2G, 3G, and 4G technologies. SEPs are patents that are essential to implement a technical standard, such as GSM, CDMA, or LTE, and the patent owners are required to license them on fair, reasonable, and non-discriminatory (FRAND) terms. Ericsson claimed that the Indian manufacturers had used its SEPs without paying the royalty fees, and sought injunctions and damages from them. The cases were heard by the Delhi High Court, which granted interim orders in favor of Ericsson and directed the Indian manufacturers to pay the royalty fees as per the

FRAND terms. The cases were later settled out of court, with the Indian manufacturers agreeing to pay the royalty fees to Ericsson. Ericsson enforced its SEPs and secured its royalty income from the Indian market, which was one of the largest and fastest-growing markets for mobile phones.

The cost of hiring a patent agent or attorney for drafting, novelty search, response to FER, and hearing would have been much lower than the potential revenue from the SEPs, which was **estimated to be around 600 million USD per year.**

These cases show that getting a patent in India for an invention can provide a high ROI for the inventor, if the invention is novel, inventive, and useful, and if the patent is valid, enforceable, and profitable.

First meeting with patent attorney

It always start with a Non disclosure agreement (NDA).

A non disclosure agreement is and agreement that patent agent / attorney or Intellectual Property firm is doing with you, to protect the confidentiality of your invention.

In other words the patent professional doing this non disclosure agreement with you (inventor) and agreeing on keeping your invention confidential / secret and do not misuse it.

There are **no cost** or charges for doing this agreement, however it is a strong document which you can take it to court your invention is misused by the patent professional (but this almost never happens)

The first meeting with patent agent or attorney could be you meeting patent attorney personally or your communication on call or via emails. The first always remains same, signing Non disclosure agreement with inventor to keep the invention confidential.

to have an effective first meeting with patent professional you should be ready with:
- [ ] a detailed description of invention where every aspect of it is completely captured
- [ ] Diagrams, flowcharts and illustrations if applicable
- [ ] comprehensive list of keywords, synonyms and search terms
- [ ] list of closest possible prior arts
- [ ] differences and problems with prior arts that our invention is solving
- [ ] other products or services in market that are similar to our invention
- [ ] our competitor working in same field
- [ ] what feature is novel and non obvious
- [ ] commercially important feature to protect
- [ ] sample claims from your point of view

and all the relevant answers to question from Indention disclosure form

and that's where **our idea incubation phase** helps us to be well prepared and ahead of time while contacting patent agent / attorney for the first time.

Thus it becomes an easy job for us now... all we need to do is share the outcome documents that we have prepared from the idea incubation phase along with the closest possible prior arts that we have identified.

Ideally Patent agent or attorney would like to go through all this information before having meeting with you such that the meeting becomes fruitful and result oriented.

It is important for you to understand that all the information that is relevant to the innovative ideas should be disclosed to the patent attorney sometimes seemingly un-important or trivial information **could prove important** in the context of the invention.

Sometimes patent attorney might ask you to illustrate **entire timeline starting with Idea** and the action steps that you took to develop the innovative idea into current state, this time line discussion also includes technical details of the invention, its features and advantages, What problem invention solve, and how it is different or better than prior arts already known to public.

Another important aspect of this first meeting with patent attorney is to get **working invention disclosure** having sufficient information about the innovative idea such that it becomes enabling, and person skilled in the art would be able to practice their invention based on the disclosure. And with the detailed invention disclosure patent professional could perform the comprehensive Novelty / Patentability search.

it is important to discuss all the **synonyms** and different set of **keywords used to identify the same element** of the invention, here again or preparation that we did in Idea incubation phase comes to rescue and we are already ready with all the synonyms and parallel words used for different elements of our invention. Many times it is important for patent attorney to understand whether the elements of the invention could be replaced with something similar and still the performs its intended purpose?

It is important to list down all such elements that could be replaced so as to form the highest possible protection while writing claims and detailed description of the invention. as a part of discussion during first meeting with patent attorney you might be asked to differentiate your invention in reference to prior arts. you may be asked for identifying the novel feature or novel part of the invention along with identifying commercially important element of the invention. patent attorney labels a reference number to your invention disclosure for further communication and keeping all the records organized.

Drafting the first claim in the meeting itself

If we have performed all the steps correctly tin now, and have communicated all results to patent agent or attorney before the meeting for review (of course after signing NDA online or via email) then this step is possible.

A patent claim is a legal statement that defines the scope and content of a patent. It is the most important part of a patent application, as it determines what the inventor can exclude others from making, using, selling, or importing. A patent claim should be clear, concise, complete, and consistent, and should comply with the patent law and practice of the country where the patent application is filed.

It would be really helpful if a patent attorney could draft the first claim (first independent claim) for your invention during the first meeting itself, as most of the description in the patent application follows the claims, it would be a great achievement if you and patent agent or attorney could write the first set of claims in the first meeting itself. Of course the claim would be revised and updated but if we could get finalized set of at least first independent claim in first meeting itself when you (and patent attorney) is together then this would be a great head start for moving towards filing patent application for your invention.

This step will **greatly enhance the speed** of completing patent application as having finalized set of claims ready will make the job of writing the patent application easier and less time consuming.

4. Patentability search or Novelty search

This would be a comprehensive search performed by patent practitioners to find out patentability of your innovative idea. Similar to the brief preliminary search that we have performed in the idea incubation phase, this search also have the objective to find out the closest possible prior art related to our invention.

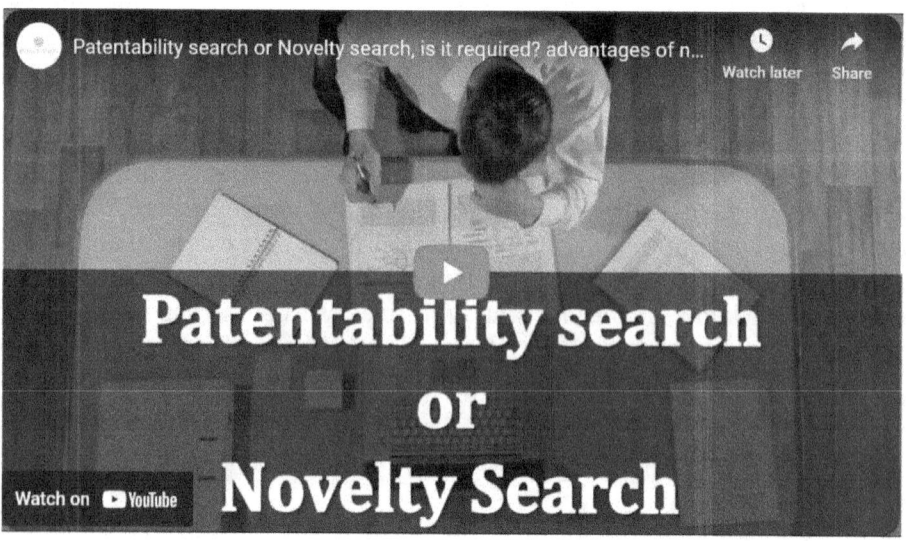

Link to the video

but unlike our brief search the patent practitioner goes into most comprehensive and detailed search as possible. The patentability search involves

---

The patentability search involves

- ☐ advance keyword search tactics
- ☐ classification search
- ☐ search by company name or assignee
- ☐ combination of different strategies in a single search query
- ☐ searching forward and backward referenced of a good prior art
- ☐ search in different patent databases
- ☐ Patent applications that are published
- ☐ Patents that are granted
- ☐ non-patent literature like articles blogs websites
- ☐ IEEE papers and non patent literature search
- ☐ products and services available in market
- ☐ and other relevant the platforms in the domain of your invention

---

The patentability search is aimed towards finding out the novelty and non-obviousness of the invention, the search identifies the closes possible prior arts (known to the public) relating to your invention, and based on the results obtained an opinion about the patentability of your invention may be provided by a patent agent or attorney. The patentability opinion may be positive, negative, or neutral.

A positive patentability opinion indicates you stand a good chance to get your patent granted for your invention. This search (novelty or patentability) saves us from filing a patent for an invention for which 100% overlapping prior arts are readily available to the public. in such cases, the patentability search would give a negative opinion. The patentability report and opinion help you decide whether to go ahead with the filing of a patent or not, chances are what you thought as a novel might already have been patented or known to the public.

In the report the results of this patentability search are closely analyzed and map against the elements of our invention. It is important responsibility of inventor to help patent attorney to identify how our invention is different and or improved from the results that are cited in the patentability search report.

Ideal case would be some aspect of our invention is are solving a long standing problem that the prior art patents failed to solve. This would prove a strong evidence to prove non obviousness of our invention

Novelty search or patentability search report saves lots of time, effort and cost for you preventing you from filing an invention that is not Novel. therefore although optional it is a recommended step in the patent procedure. Detailed article about this step "Patentability search or Novelty search"

Costs: the attorney fee for performing a patentability or novelty search is ₹ 15,000. or (USD 180)

Time: the time required is about 5-7 working days

Opinion on patentability

Based on the result on patentability search patent attorney give an opinion about the patentability of your innovative idea:

- **Negative opinion:** If there are results in patentability search report which are similar to your invention and there is no novelty in your innovative idea compared to existing knowledge. That is the innovative idea is already known to public and there is no novelty. then a patent agent or attorney might advise you not to go for patent filing as your innovative idea is lacking novelty. This will save you a lot of time and costs that you otherwise would be incurring on filing patent application for an idea which would not result in granted patent.

- **Neutral opinion:** in this case the patent agent / attorney is of opinion that your invention stands a fair chance of winning patent for some aspects of your invention which are found to be novel and having inventive step based on results in patentability search. You may receive some objections from patent office yet by responding to it you may get patent for your invention.

- **Positive opinion:** this is when your invention has some features that are novel and non obvious that is seems to be having inventive step when compared with existing knowledge and prior arts found in the patentability report. This is a positive sign and patent agent or attorney might advise you to go ahead for patent filing.

Advantages of patentability search

☐ Patentability search help us in identifying the closest possible prior arts which are likely to be found by examiner at the examination stage of the patent application. Hence considering these prior art before writing patent application **increase chances of getting patent granted**.

☐ The identified prior arts are mentioned in the references and our invention is established as solution to long standing problem which is not yet solved. such an approach creates good chances of proving inventive step that is the solution our invention has provided was not obvious to a person skilled in the art as the problem is existed for so long. Hence it is

useful in proving novelty and inventive step which improves chances of getting patent granted for our invention.

☐ And ultimately patentability search also **saves lot of unnecessary costs**, efforts and procedures in filing the patent application for invention which doesn't stand a chance of surviving patentability criteria and would be rejected anyway.

5. Preparing Patent application (patent drafting)

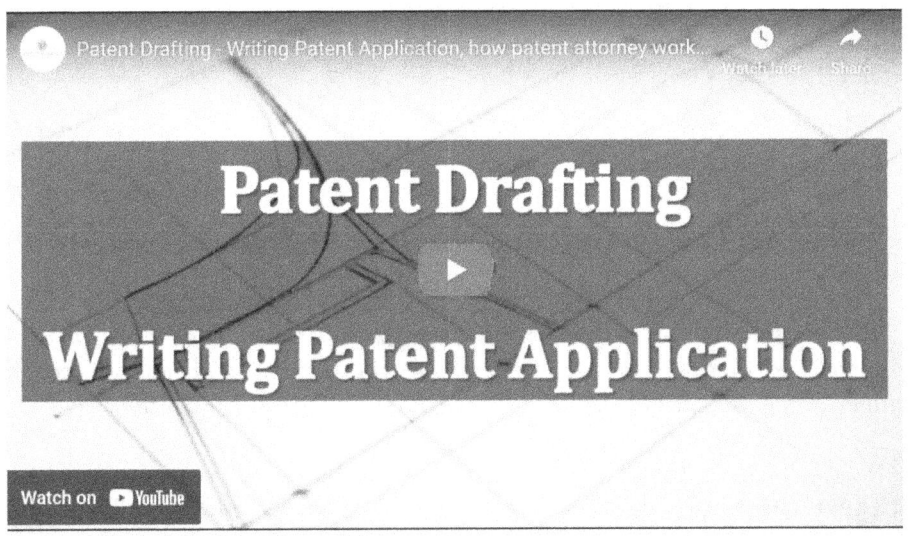

Link for video

Let's review our expectation from a patent application one more time.

The outcome expected from Patent protection

✓ Provide broadest possible protection to our innovative ideas
✓ Competitors should not be able to copy or compete with our invention without our consent
✓ Competitors should not be able to work around our patented invention and build similar solution without infringing on our patent (this is most important point)
✓ we should be able to monetize the patented invention by
    o   by producing patented invention without competition
    o   by licensing it to other company to get royalty payments
    o   by completely selling the patent rights to other business
and get significant monetary benefits for your efforts

---

writing a patent application around the novel feature of the invention which has inventive step needs very balanced and scientific approach.

Going too broad or too narrow protection while writing claims would be a mistake.

"Claims should not be too broad because those would be anticipated by existing prior arts, and the claims should not be too narrow because competitors would not be able to work around and use our invention"

Now as an inventor or applicant of patent **you are not supposed to know all these rule and skills for patent drafting**, so we would be brief about this. As the sole purpose of this book is to educate you with all the steps involved and mistakes to avoid, cares to take at every stage.

So we would not going in to much details of the patent drafting, and how it is done as we are not teaching inventors to draft patent application, which would be really difficult to achieve with a book or let alone single chapter in a book.

The purpose of this section is to **make you (inventor) aware** about what happens at every stage, behind the scene actions happing with your invention disclosure and what to expect at each stage.

We will start form where we left of the last section on patentability opinion. after receiving neutral or positive patentability opinion form patent agent / attorney, you take a decision whether to proceed with the patent drafting and patent filing process.

Depending up on:
- □ the type of patent application (provisional or complete)
- □ complexity of subject matter
- □ preparedness of inventor with required information (invention disclosure) and
- □ time / bandwidth available to work on your project (along with other projects)

it takes about 5 to 12 days for a patent agent or patent attorney to come up with a draft of patent application, which you review along with him.

Patent drafting how patent professional does it

You may be surprised to know, the patent drafting does not begin with title of the invention or the abstract; In fact most patent professional first draft claims !!!

Claims are most important part of patent application.

❑ Claims decide the boundaries of the protection that you would be getting for your invention
❑ Claims are used to enforce your patent
❑ Claims decide whether the competitor is infringing on your patent
❑ Claim are closely examined in the patent examination phase at patent office
❑ Claims are most difficult part of patent application to write

Of course, there are other dependencies and rules for other parts of patent applications when deciding scope but it is the claim which stands most important thing that decides the future of your patent.

Important things about claims:

The purpose of claim is to define the invention protected by the patent.

The reason patent agent or attorney starts with writing claims first, because once we have complete set of claims providing appropriate protection to the invention and which are approved by you (inventor), then writing remaining parts of the patent application like: detailed description, abstract and summary becomes easier as these parts generally follow the boundaries set by claims.

How to review claims

To be honest, a patent agent or attorney is the most appropriate person to write and review claims with you, however there are some important things to consider :

☐ Since, claims define the scope of legal protection, it is suggested that they should be drafted carefully to cover all the aspects of the protection being sought at the same time adequately distinguishing the prior art from the claimed invention.
☐ Unity of invention and clarity of claims
  ○ a) Claim(s) of a Complete Specification shall relate to a single invention, or to a group of inventions linked so as to form a

single inventive concept.
- o b) Claims shall be clear and succinct and fairly based on the matter disclosed in the specification.
- □ Significance of Claims
  - o a) A claim is a statement of technical facts expressed in legal terms defining the scope of the invention sought to be protected. No exclusivity is obtained for any matter described in the Complete
  Specification unless it is claimed in the claim
- □ What is not claimed in the claims stands disclaimed, and is open to public use, even if the matter is disclosed in the description.
- □ Each claim is evaluated on its own merit and, therefore, if one of the claims is objected, it does not mean that the rest of the claims are invalid. It is therefore important to make claims on all aspects of the invention to ensure that the applicant gets the widest possible protection.

And there are many rules and standard practices that a professional would be incorporating while writing claims for your patent application. In short,

"Claims should be written in such a way that they would not be invalidated in the litigation phase and they would not allow competitors to practice the invention without infringing on patented invention"

Just like claims, there are many rules and standards for writing other elements of patent specification like:

- Detailed description of the invention
- Diagrams, illustrations and images
- Abstract
- Field of invention
- Background of the invention
- Include references to cite
- Title of the invention
- disclosing best mode
- covering all possible embodiments

and many more…

however discussing all the rules and regulation is outside the scope of this book and its outcome. Still if you are interested in reading them, below are the documents on government patent office website you can download and read…

The Patents Act 1970	**The Patents Rules 2003**	**Manual of Patent office Practice and Procedure**

http://www.ipindia.nic.in/ website under resources section

Acts	Rules	Manuals	Guidelines
› Patents	› Patents	› Patents	› Patents
› Designs	› Designs	› Designs	› Trade Marks
› Trade Mark	› Trade Mark	› Trade Marks	› Geographical Indications
› Geographical Indications	› Geographical Indications	› Geographical Indications	

How patent attorney works on your invention

when you think about near perfect patent application that properly protect your invention, there are few things a patent application should do:

- ☐ The claims for invention written in appropriate manner such that claims are broad enough to stop competitors from working around the invention and at the same time claims are narrow enough not to be anticipated by existing prior art
- ☐ Describing the invention in enough detailed manner such that the person skilled in the art should be able to understand and practice the invention, that is it should be enabling description of the invention.
- ☐ all possible variation and embodiments of the invention are covered.
- ☐ claiming the invention in such a way that it will survive not only prosecution (that is till the grant) but also it will survive the litigation phase (after the grant). And licensing phase (that is making money with patented invention)
- ☐ describing the best mode of practicing the invention
- ☐ and in case you (inventor) decides to go for foreign filing a patent application should be able to facilitate foreign filing/ international filing.
- ☐ and of course the patent application should be following all the rules and laws about how patent application should be written as required by patent law.

based on all of these input the patent attorney creates the final draft of the patent application along with the drawings to be reviewed by inventor. And upon receiving the final draft of the patent application you (inventor) should review it line by line keeping in mind the scope of your invention that you want to be protected.

all the corrections that is adding information removing information or editing existing information is to be done with track changes enabled document editor, search that your corrections would be appropriately grasped by patent agent or attorney. and after considering suggestions and changes the patent application is ready to be filed in patent office.

Proactively speeding up the process

There are different strategies to speed up the process from idea to granted patent.

- being ready with appropriate information about the invention really reduces time from ideation stage of invention to patent filed stage of invention, Idea incubation phase and preliminary search help in great deal to speed things up and shorten the time and frequency of communication with patent professional
- another strategy would drafting first claim in the meeting with patent agent or attorney which helps in creating rest of the patent application in quicker time. Saving a lot of emails and meetings for same outcome.
- Directly filing complete patent application, without spending time in patentability search or provisional patent application
- After filing the patent application, you can file early publication request in patent office using form 9 and paying prescribed fees (which is Rs. 2500 for individual inventor). By doing this you need not wait for the expiry of 18 months from the filing date of the patent application and controller publishes your application as soon as possible.
- Immediately after the application is published filing request for examination (RFE) in form 18 and with fees 4000 for individual inventor.
- Expedited examination of applications can be made as per rule 24 C with form 18 A provided (a) that India has been indicated as the competent International Searching Authority or elected as an International Preliminary Examining Authority in the corresponding international application; or (b) that the applicant is a startup.
- And responding to objections raised by controller in least possible time

Another approach is going for Expedited examination (faster) route : We will learn it in important section explaining Expedited examination route and how it would speed up the process for grant of patent.

6. Patent drafting - Patent writing Guidelines

Let's quickly go through each part of patent application and try to understand it.

Section	Purpose	Guidelines
Title of the Invention	Provides a concise summary of the invention.	Keep it brief and descriptive. Avoid technical jargon and overly broad terms.
Field of the Invention	Identifies the technical field of the invention.	Be specific but not too narrow. Use commonly understood terms.
Background of the Invention	Offers context about existing solutions and their limits.	Describe the problem your invention solves and how current solutions are inadequate.
Summary of the Invention	Gives a brief overview of the invention and its benefits.	Summarize the invention's purpose, main features, and advantages. Clear and concise.
Objects of the Invention	Outlines the specific goals or problems addressed.	Clearly state the objectives, emphasizing practical utility and relevance.
Brief Description of Drawings	Explains each drawing or figure.	Provide a clear description of each drawing, ensuring correlation with the detailed description.
Detailed Description of the Invention	Offers an in-depth explanation of the invention.	Be comprehensive and detailed. Describe every component and function in clear language.
Claims	Defines the scope of protection sought.	Start with broader claims, then move to specific ones. Ensure clarity and precision.
Abstract	Provides a snapshot of the invention for quick overview.	Keep it brief, ideally under 150 words. Concisely summarize key aspects and utility.

Title of the Invention

When it comes to drafting a patent application, the title plays an essential and often underestimated role. In accordance with the Indian Patent Act, the title of a patent application should be a clear and concise indicator of the nature of the invention.

This section delves into the best practices for choosing an effective title, backed by the guidelines of the Indian Patent Act, and underscores its importance in the patentability process.

The Importance of a Good Title: A well-chosen title serves several key purposes:

- Identification: It helps in easily identifying and categorizing the invention in patent databases.
- First Impression: It provides the first glimpse of the invention to examiners and the public, setting the tone for the understanding of the patent.
- Legal Compliance: An accurately descriptive title is a requirement under the Indian Patent Act, which can impact the patent's validity.

Choosing an Effective Title:

1. Descriptive Nature: The title should directly reflect the essence of the invention. For instance, a patent for a new type of solar panel could be titled "High-Efficiency Photovoltaic Solar Panel." This is descriptive and immediately informs the reader about the nature of the invention.
2. Brevity and Clarity: A title should be concise yet informative. It should avoid being overly technical, while still clearly indicating the invention's purpose.
3. Avoiding Ambiguity: Vague titles can be misleading. For example, a title like "New Improvement" is too broad and does not inform about the invention's specific nature.
4. No Promotional Language: The title should not contain adjectives that promote the invention, such as "Advanced" or "Best." It should remain neutral and factual.

5. Technical Terms: While the use of technical terms is acceptable, they should be commonly understood in the field of the invention. Jargon that is too esoteric might confuse rather than clarify.

Legal Considerations: Under the Indian Patent Act, the title should not be changed in a manner that alters the invention's nature post-submission. This highlights the importance of getting the title right from the outset. A misleading or inaccurate title can lead to issues during the patent examination process, potentially impacting the patent's validity or scope.

An effective title is not just a label; it's a critical component of the patent application. It should be thoughtfully crafted to accurately represent the invention, complying with the legal requirements of the Indian Patent Act. A good title aids in the clear identification and understanding of the invention, playing a significant role in the patent's journey through the examination process and its subsequent impact in the relevant field.

For example: a good title for an invention related to a smart watch with health monitoring features could be "Smart Watch with Integrated Electrocardiogram Sensor".

Field of the Invention

Defining the 'Field of the Invention' is a crucial aspect of drafting a patent application, especially in the context of the Indian patent system. This section of the application not only helps in situating the invention within a specific technological area but also plays a significant role in the patent examination process.

Why is the Field of the Invention Important?
1. Contextual Clarity: It provides patent examiners and readers with immediate context about the technical realm of the invention.
2. Facilitates Patent Classification: Correct classification of the patent is crucial for its examination process, and this classification is greatly influenced by the field of the invention.
3. Aids in Prior Art Search: A well-defined field can streamline the process of searching for prior art, ensuring that relevant technologies are considered during examination.

Identifying the Appropriate Field:

1. Understand Your Invention: Analyze the primary function and technological area of your invention. For instance, a new type of battery technology would likely fall under the field of 'Electrochemical Energy Storage Technologies.'
2. Use Broad Terms Wisely: While the field should be specific, it should not be so narrow as to exclude relevant technological areas. Broad terms should be used strategically to encompass the invention's scope.
3. Reference Industry Standards: Look at how similar inventions are categorized and use industry-standard terms to describe your field.

Impact on Patent Classification and Examination:

- Correct Examiner Assignment: The field of the invention helps in assigning the application to an examiner with the right expertise, which can influence the thoroughness and outcome of the examination.
- Comparison with Prior Art: By accurately defining the field, you help ensure that the invention is compared against the most relevant existing technologies during the examination.

Legal Aspects as per the Indian Patent Manual: According to the Indian Patent Manual, the field of the invention should be clearly and precisely stated. This helps in meeting the requirements of the Indian Patent Act, which emphasizes the need for clarity and specificity in patent applications.

The 'Field of the Invention' is more than just a formal requirement; it's a fundamental part of your patent application that affects its processing and examination. By accurately defining this field, you not only adhere to the guidelines of the Indian Patent Manual but also enhance the chances of your patent being correctly evaluated and granted.

For example: a good field of invention for the same invention could be "The present invention relates to smart watches, and more particularly, to smart watches with health monitoring features."

Background of the Invention

The 'Background of the Invention' is a critical section in a patent application, particularly under the Indian patent system. This part of the document sets the stage for understanding the invention by providing context about the existing state of technology and the specific problem the invention aims to solve.

The Role and Significance of Background Information:
1. Establishing the Need for the Invention: The background helps to identify the deficiencies or limitations in the current state of technology, demonstrating the need for the invention.
2. Highlighting the Invention's Novelty: By contrasting the invention against the backdrop of existing technology, the background section can underscore the novelty and inventive step of the invention.
3. Aiding Patent Examiners and Judges: A well-written background provides patent examiners and, in the event of litigation, judges, with a clear understanding of the technical field and the problems addressed by the invention.

Guidelines for Writing the Background Section:

1. Describe the Current State of Art: Start by outlining the existing technologies, processes, or products related to your invention. Be factual and objective in your description.
2. Identify the Problems or Limitations: Clearly articulate the problems or limitations of the current technologies or methods. This could be inefficiencies, cost issues, technical limitations, or any other relevant shortcomings.
3. Reference Prior Art: Where applicable, reference specific examples of prior art (previous patents, published articles, etc.) that relate to your invention. This helps in establishing the existing knowledge base against which your invention is an improvement.

Structuring the Background Section:

- Organized and Logical Flow: Present the information in a logical sequence, starting from the general state of the art and gradually narrowing down to the specific problems your invention addresses.
- Avoid Negative Language: While highlighting limitations, avoid disparaging or negative language about existing solutions. Focus on the limitations rather than the solutions themselves.

Legal Considerations in the Indian Context: Under the Indian patent system, the background of the invention must not only be informative but also align with legal standards. It should not overstate the invention's capabilities or understate the effectiveness of existing solutions. Misrepresentation in this section can lead to challenges in the patent's validity.

The 'Background of the Invention' is more than just a historical account of existing technologies; it is a strategic narrative that positions your invention within the larger technological landscape. By effectively articulating the problems with current technologies and how your invention addresses them, you set a strong foundation for demonstrating the novelty and utility of your invention under the Indian patent system.

For example, a good background of invention for the same invention could be "Smart watches are wearable devices that can perform various functions, such as displaying time, date, weather, notifications, messages, calls, etc., and connecting with other devices, such as smartphones, tablets, computers, etc. Some smart watches also have health monitoring features, such as measuring and displaying the blood pressure, blood oxygen level, body temperature, etc., of the user. However, most of these smart watches do not have the ability to measure and display the electrocardiogram (ECG) of the user, which is an important indicator of the cardiac health and function of the user. ECG is a graphical representation of the electrical activity of the heart, which can show the heart rate, rhythm, and any abnormalities, such as arrhythmia, ischemia, infarction, etc. ECG can help to diagnose and prevent various cardiac diseases and emergencies, such as heart attack, stroke, cardiac arrest, etc. However, conventional ECG devices are bulky, expensive, and invasive, and require the user to attach electrodes to different parts of the body, such as the chest, arms, and legs, and to visit a hospital or a clinic for the test. Therefore, there is a need for a smart watch that can measure and display the ECG of the user in a convenient and non-invasive way, and alert the user or a third party in case of any abnormality."

Summary of the Invention

The 'Summary of the Invention' is a pivotal section in a patent application, especially within the framework of the Indian Patent Rules. Unlike the abstract, which offers a brief snapshot of the invention, the Summary provides a more detailed overview, elucidating the invention's purpose, key features, and advantages.

The Role and Purpose of the Summary:
1. Expanding on the Abstract: While the abstract is a succinct overview, the Summary delves deeper, offering more detail about the invention's technical aspects and its advantages.
2. Facilitating Understanding: This section helps readers, especially patent examiners, quickly grasp the essence of the invention, its functionality, and its potential applications.

Drafting the Summary:
1. Describe Key Features: Outline the primary components or steps of your invention. Highlight what makes your invention unique compared to existing technologies.
2. Explain Advantages: Clearly articulate the benefits or improvements your invention offers. This could include increased efficiency, cost-effectiveness, technical advancements, etc.
3. Keep It Accessible: While more detailed than the abstract, the Summary should still be easily understandable to someone familiar with the field but not necessarily an expert.

Differentiating from the Abstract:
- Length and Detail: The Summary is typically longer and more detailed than the abstract. It provides enough information to understand the invention's novelty without delving into the detailed technical aspects.

- Focus on Innovation: The Summary should emphasize the innovative aspects of your invention, explaining how it improves upon or differs from existing solutions.

Legal Considerations under Indian Patent Rules:

- Consistency with Claims: The Summary should be consistent with the claims and detailed description, accurately reflecting the scope of the invention.
- No Overstatements: Avoid overpromising or overstating the capabilities of your invention. Misleading information in the Summary can lead to legal issues later.

The 'Summary of the Invention' is an integral part of a patent application, providing a bridge between the concise abstract and the detailed description. A well-drafted Summary not only aids in the understanding of the invention but also highlights its significance and novelty. Under the Indian Patent Rules, this section should be clear, informative, and reflective of the invention's true nature and scope.

For example, a good summary of invention for the same invention could be "The present invention provides a smart watch with an integrated electrocardiogram sensor that can measure and display the heart rate and rhythm of the user, and alert the user or a third party in case of any abnormality. The smart watch comprises a display unit, a processor unit, a communication unit, a power unit, and a sensor unit. The sensor unit includes an electrocardiogram sensor that is attached to the wristband of the smart watch and contacts the skin of the user. The sensor unit collects and transmits the electrocardiogram signals to the processor unit, which analyzes and displays the results on the display unit, and sends a notification to the communication unit if necessary. The smart watch provides a convenient and non-invasive way of monitoring the cardiac health of the user, and can prevent or reduce the risk of cardiac diseases and emergencies. As used herein, the term 'electrocardiogram sensor' means a device that can detect and measure the electrical activity of the heart, and generate an electrocardiogram signal. The term 'display unit' means a device that can show the time, date, weather, notifications, messages, calls, etc., and the electrocardiogram results of the user. The term 'processor unit' means a device that can receive, process, analyze, and store the electrocardiogram signals and other data from the sensor unit and the communication unit, and control the display unit and the communication unit. The term 'communication unit' means a device that can connect with other devices, such as smartphones, tablets, computers, etc., and send and receive data, such as electrocardiogram results, notifications, messages, calls, etc. The term 'power unit' means a device that can supply and manage the power for the smart watch and its components."

Objects of the Invention

In the context of drafting a patent application, the 'Objects of the Invention' section plays a crucial role, particularly in the Indian patent framework. This section is dedicated to explicitly stating the objectives, aims, or goals of the invention, which is vital for several reasons.

Purpose and Significance of the Objects of the Invention:
1. Clarifying Intent: This section makes clear the intention behind the invention, outlining what it seeks to achieve or solve.
2. Guiding the Interpretation of Claims: The objectives can help in interpreting the scope and breadth of the claims. It provides a context for understanding how the invention is intended to be used or applied.
3. Demonstrating Utility: By articulating the objectives, this section underscores the practical utility of the invention, a key requirement for patentability.

Drafting the Objects of the Invention:

1. Be Specific and Direct: Clearly articulate specific problems or limitations in existing technologies that your invention addresses. For instance, if the invention is a new type of solar panel, its objects might include improved energy efficiency and reduced manufacturing costs.
2. Highlight Novelty and Advantages: Use this section to emphasize how your invention is different from and superior to existing solutions. However, ensure that these claims are realistic and supported by your invention.
3. Align with the Overall Application: The objectives should be consistent with the rest of your patent application, especially the detailed description and claims.

Unlike the 'Summary of the Invention' or the 'Detailed Description,' the 'Objects of the Invention' is less about technical details and more about the invention's intended purpose and its practical implications.

Legal Considerations in the Indian Context:
- In line with the Indian Patent Act and Manual, the objectives of the invention should not be misleading or overly broad. They should be realistically achievable by the invention as disclosed.
- The stated objectives can play a crucial role during patent prosecution and potential litigation, as they offer insights into the inventor's intent and the invention's intended use.

Defining the 'Objects of the Invention' is a critical step in contextualizing your invention within a patent application. This section not only clarifies the purpose and practical applicability of your invention but also supports the narrative of novelty and utility crucial for patentability. In the Indian patent system, it's essential to articulate these objectives clearly, realistically, and in alignment with the rest of the application to ensure a strong and enforceable patent.

Brief Description of Drawings

In patent applications, particularly under the Indian Patent System, the 'Brief Description of Drawings' section plays a significant role in enhancing the understanding of the invention. This part of the application, guided by the Indian Patent Manual, is where the inventor explains what each drawing, figure, or diagram in the application illustrates.

Importance of Describing Drawings:
1. Visual Clarification: Drawings can often convey complex aspects of an invention more clearly than words. The brief descriptions help in interpreting these drawings correctly.
2. Supplementing the Written Description: They serve to complement the detailed written description of the invention, providing a visual guide that can make understanding the invention easier and more intuitive.

3. Legal Requirement: Including a brief description of each drawing is a legal requirement under the Indian patent system and helps ensure that the patent application is comprehensive.

Best Practices for Describing Drawings:
1. Label Each Drawing: Start by labeling each figure or drawing (e.g., Figure 1, Figure 2) and reference these labels in your description.
2. Be Concise but Descriptive: For each drawing, provide a concise explanation of what is shown. Focus on the key elements that are relevant to understanding the invention.
3. Sequence the Descriptions Logically: Follow the same order in your descriptions as in the drawings. If the drawings depict a process or a series of steps, describe them in the order they occur.
4. Reference the Detailed Description: Where applicable, refer to the detailed description of the invention for more comprehensive information.

The descriptions act as a bridge, connecting the visual information in the drawings with the technical details in the text. They help clarify how different parts of the invention function or fit together, which can be crucial for complex inventions.

Legal Considerations:
- As per the Indian Patent Manual, each drawing should be accompanied by a brief explanation. Failure to adequately describe the drawings can lead to ambiguity, which can impact the patent's validity or scope.
- The descriptions should be accurate and should not introduce inconsistencies with the rest of the application.

The 'Brief Description of Drawings' is an integral part of a patent application, especially in the visual communication of the invention. Effective descriptions enhance the reader's understanding and ensure that the drawings serve their intended purpose of clarifying and complementing the written text. Under the Indian Patent System, adhering to these best practices is not only beneficial for the clarity of the application but also a legal necessity for a complete and enforceable patent.

For example: a good brief description of drawings for the same invention could be "The patent drawings illustrate the preferred embodiment of the present invention, and are not intended to limit the scope of the invention. In the drawings: FIG. 1 is a front view of the smart watch according to the present invention; FIG. 2 is a back view of the smart watch according to the present invention; FIG. 3 is a side view of the smart watch according to the present invention; FIG. 4 is a block diagram of the smart watch according to the present invention; FIG. 5 is a schematic diagram of the electrocardiogram sensor according to the present invention; FIG. 6 is a flowchart of the method of measuring and displaying the electrocardiogram of the user according to the present invention. In the drawings, the reference signs and their meanings are as follows: 10: smart watch; 11: display unit; 12: processor unit; 13: communication unit; 14: power unit; 15: sensor unit; 16: electrocardiogram sensor; 17: wristband; 18: skin; 19: electrocardiogram signal; 20: electrocardiogram result; 21: notification."

Detailed Description of the Invention

The 'Detailed Description of the Invention' is a fundamental component of a patent application, particularly in the Indian patent regime. This section requires a comprehensive explanation of the invention, elaborating on every aspect to ensure that the invention is fully understood and can be effectively implemented by someone skilled in the relevant field.

Purpose of the Detailed Description:
1. Elucidating the Invention: It provides a thorough explanation of the invention, including its construction, operation, and possible variations.
2. Support for Claims: The detailed description is the bedrock upon which the claims are based. It must contain sufficient detail to support each claim made in the patent application.

Process of Writing the Detailed Description:
1. Comprehensive Coverage: Start by explaining all the components or elements of your invention. Describe how these components interact and work together to achieve the desired outcome.
2. Include Variants and Alternatives: Discuss possible variations of the invention or alternative ways it can be implemented. This helps in broadening the scope of the patent protection.

3. Use Clear and Concise Language: Avoid overly technical jargon that could make the invention difficult to understand. The language should be clear enough for someone in the relevant field to replicate the invention.

4. Step-by-Step Explanation: If the invention involves a process, describe each step in detail. Clarify the sequence and interaction of steps where necessary.

5. Reference the Drawings: Relate the description back to the drawings, providing a clear link between the visual representations and the textual description.

Level of Detail Required:

- The level of detail must be sufficient for a person skilled in the relevant field to understand and replicate the invention without undue experimentation.
- Avoid leaving out critical details that are essential for the functionality of the invention.

How This Section Supports the Claims:

- The detailed description provides the technical foundation for the claims. Each element or feature mentioned in the claims should be clearly described in this section.
- A well-written detailed description can prevent the claims from being interpreted as overly broad or vague.

Legal Considerations in the Indian Context:

- Under the Indian Patent Act and Rules, the detailed description must disclose the best method of performing the invention known to the applicant.
- Failure to adequately describe the invention can lead to the rejection of the patent application or challenges to its validity.

The 'Detailed Description of the Invention' is where the inventor gets to explain their invention in full. This section is not just a technical requirement; it is an opportunity to showcase the invention in its entirety, reinforcing the claims and ensuring that the patent application meets the stringent requirements of the Indian patent system. A meticulous and thorough description can significantly enhance the strength and scope of the patent protection granted.

Detailed Description of Invention: This is a section that describes the detailed structure, function, operation, and embodiment of your invention, and supports the patent claims. It should provide a clear and complete disclosure of your invention, and explain how your invention solves the technical problem and achieves the technical advantage. It should also describe the best mode of carrying out the invention, and any variations, modifications, or alternatives of the invention that are within the scope of the invention. It should include examples and embodiments of your invention, and refer to the patent drawings and the reference signs to illustrate and clarify your invention. It should not include any information or features that are not relevant or essential to your invention, or that are already known in the prior art. For example, a good detailed description of invention for the same invention could be "The present invention will now be described in detail with reference to the accompanying drawings. FIG

Writing Claims for Patent

In a patent application, the 'Claims' section is arguably the most critical part, especially under the Indian Patent Act. This section legally defines the scope of protection that is granted by the patent. Writing clear, precise, and enforceable claims is essential for securing and maintaining robust patent protection.

The Role of Claims in a Patent Application:
1. Defining Legal Boundaries: Claims determine what is and isn't protected by the patent. They set the legal boundaries of the invention.
2. Guide for Enforcement: The strength and enforceability of a patent largely depend on how well the claims are drafted. They are the primary reference in any legal dispute regarding patent infringement.

Process of Writing Effective Claims:
1. Start Broad, Then Get Specific: Begin with broader claims to cover as much ground as possible, then proceed to more specific claims to cover specific embodiments of the invention.
2. Clarity and Conciseness: Claims should be clear and to the point. Avoid ambiguous language that could lead to misinterpretation.
3. Technical Accuracy: Ensure that the technical aspects of the claims are accurate and fully supported by the detailed description.

4. Include Different Types of Claims: If applicable, include independent and dependent claims. Independent claims stand on their own, while dependent claims refer back to and further specify the independent claims.

Importance of Scope and Specificity:
- Scope: The scope of the claims should be broad enough to provide meaningful protection but not so broad that they become invalid due to lack of novelty or obviousness.
- Specificity: Claims must be specific enough to clearly differentiate the invention from prior art. This specificity helps in enforcing the patent against infringement.

Legal Considerations Under the Indian Patent Act:
- The claims must conform to the provisions of the Indian Patent Act, which requires that they are clear, succinct, and supported by the description.
- They must define the matter for which protection is sought in terms of the technical features of the invention.

Formulating the claims is a nuanced process that requires a balance between breadth, specificity, and legal compliance. In the context of the Indian patent system, well-crafted claims not only define the scope of protection but also enhance the enforceability of the patent. Clear, precise, and well-supported claims are instrumental in securing a strong legal position for the inventor, both during the patent examination process and in any subsequent legal disputes.

Patent claims are the legal statements that define the scope and content of your patent. They are the most important part of your patent application, as they determine what you can exclude others from making, using, selling, or importing.

Therefore, you should write your patent claims carefully and clearly, and comply with the patent law and practice of the country where you are filing. There are two main types of patent claims: independent claims and dependent claims.

An independent claim is a patent claim that does not refer to any other claims and stands on its own. A dependent claim, on the other hand, depends on and refers to another claim and incorporates the entire claim or part of the claim by reference. Independent claims are usually broader and more general than dependent claims, and they cover the essential features of your invention.

Dependent claims are usually narrower and more specific than independent claims, and they add additional features or limitations to the invention. You should write at least one independent claim and one or more dependent claims for your invention, and make sure that they are clear, concise, complete, and consistent.

There are also different categories of patent claims, depending on the type of invention and the subject matter. The most common categories are product or apparatus claims, process or method claims, and use claims. Product or apparatus claims are claims that refer to a physical entity, such as a device, a machine, a system, a composition, etc. Process or method claims are claims that refer to an activity, such as a way of making, using, or doing something. Use claims are claims that refer to a specific application or purpose of a product or a process.

You should write your patent claims according to the category of your invention, and use appropriate language and terminology.

For example: product or apparatus claims usually start with "A/an [product or apparatus] comprising ...", process or method claims usually start with "A method for/of [process or method] comprising ...", and use claims usually start with "A use of [product or process] for [purpose] ...".
Here are some examples of patent claims for different types of inventions and categories, along with links to the granted patents where they are taken from:

Product or apparatus claim for a smart watch with health monitoring features:
1. A smart watch with an integrated electrocardiogram sensor that can measure and display the heart rate and rhythm of the user, and alert the user or a third party in case of any abnormality, comprising:
    - a display unit that can show the time, date, weather, notifications, messages, calls, etc., and the electrocardiogram results of the user;

- a processor unit that can receive, process, analyze, and store the electrocardiogram signals and other data from the sensor unit and the communication unit, and control the display unit and the communication unit;
- a communication unit that can connect with other devices, such as smartphones, tablets, computers, etc., and send and receive data, such as electrocardiogram results, notifications, messages, calls, etc.;
- a power unit that can supply and manage the power for the smart watch and its components; and
- a sensor unit that includes an electrocardiogram sensor that is attached to the wristband of the smart watch and contacts the skin of the user, and that collects and transmits the electrocardiogram signals to the processor unit.

2. The smart watch of claim 1, wherein the electrocardiogram sensor comprises a pair of electrodes that are spaced apart and aligned along the wristband, and that detect and measure the electrical activity of the heart.

3. The smart watch of claim 1, wherein the communication unit comprises a Bluetooth module that can pair with other Bluetooth-enabled devices, and a cellular module that can access a cellular network and make or receive calls.

Types and Formats of Claims

There are also different formats of claims, depending on the nature and category of the invention. The most common formats are:

Product or apparatus claims: These claims define the invention in terms of its structure, configuration, composition, or arrangement of components or elements. For example, a product or apparatus claim for the device that can be fitted in a vehicle to improve the fuel efficiency of the vehicle may look like this:

A device for improving the fuel efficiency of a vehicle, comprising:
- *a sensor that can detect the speed, acceleration, and deceleration of the vehicle;*

- *a controller that can receive the signals from the sensor and calculate the optimal fuel injection rate for the vehicle; and*
- *an injector that can adjust the fuel injection rate for the vehicle according to the signals from the controller.*

Method or process claims: These claims define the invention in terms of its steps, actions, operations, or functions. For example, a method or process claim for the device that can be fitted in a vehicle to improve the fuel efficiency of the vehicle may look like this:

A method for improving the fuel efficiency of a vehicle using a device, comprising the steps of:
- *detecting the speed, acceleration, and deceleration of the vehicle using a sensor;*
- *receiving the signals from the sensor and calculating the optimal fuel injection rate for the vehicle using a controller; and*
- *adjusting the fuel injection rate for the vehicle according to the signals from the controller using an injector.*

Use or application claims: These claims define the invention in terms of its purpose, function, or effect. For example, a use or application claim for the device that can be fitted in a vehicle to improve the fuel efficiency of the vehicle may look like this:
A use of a device for improving the fuel efficiency of a vehicle, wherein the device comprises:
- *a sensor that can detect the speed, acceleration, and deceleration of the vehicle;*
- *a controller that can receive the signals from the sensor and calculate the optimal fuel injection rate for the vehicle; and*
- *an injector that can adjust the fuel injection rate for the vehicle according to the signals from the controller.*

Requirements and Guidelines for Writing Claims
Claims must comply with the requirements and guidelines of the Indian Patent Office, as well as the ethical and legal standards of patentability. Some of the main requirements and guidelines are:
- Claims must be clear, concise, and supported by the detailed description and the drawings, if any. Claims must not contain vague

or ambiguous terms or expressions, such as "substantially", "approximately", "preferably", or "such as". Claims must also not contain unnecessary or redundant features or elements, such as "means for", "adapted to", or "comprising".

- Claims must be novel, inventive, and industrially applicable. Claims must not be anticipated by or obvious from the prior art, which includes any information or knowledge that is publicly available before the priority date of the patent application. Claims must also have a practical utility or benefit in any field of human activity or industry.
- Claims must be drafted in a single sentence, with proper punctuation and grammar. Claims must start with a capital letter and end with a full stop. Claims must also use appropriate transitional words or phrases, such as "comprising", "consisting of", "consisting essentially of", "characterized by", or "wherein". Claims must also use consistent terminology and definitions throughout the patent application.
- Claims must be numbered consecutively in Arabic numerals, starting from 1. Independent claims must be placed before dependent claims, and dependent claims must indicate the number of the claim or claims they depend on. Claims must also be arranged in a logical order, according to the category and format of the invention.

Steps and Strategies for Drafting Claims

Drafting claims is a skill that requires practice and experience. However, there are some general steps and strategies that can help in drafting claims for an invention for an Indian patent.

Step 1: Identify the main technical feature or the inventive concept of the invention. This is the core idea or the essence of the invention that distinguishes it from the prior art and provides the desired effect or result. For example, the main technical feature or the inventive concept of the device that can be fitted in a vehicle to improve the fuel efficiency of the vehicle may be:
The device can adjust the fuel injection rate for the vehicle according to the speed, acceleration, and deceleration of the vehicle, thereby optimizing the fuel consumption and reducing the emissions.

Step 2: Draft an independent claim that defines the invention in terms of its main technical feature or inventive concept, as well as the essential features or elements that are necessary for the invention to work. This is the broadest and most general claim that covers the scope of the invention. For example, an independent claim for the device that can be fitted in a vehicle to improve the fuel efficiency of the vehicle may look like this:

A device for improving the fuel efficiency of a vehicle, comprising:

- *a sensor that can detect the speed, acceleration, and deceleration of the vehicle;*
- *a controller that can receive the signals from the sensor and calculate the optimal fuel injection rate for the vehicle; and*
- *an injector that can adjust the fuel injection rate for the vehicle according to the signals from the controller.*

Step 3: Draft one or more dependent claims that further define the invention by adding additional features or elements that are optional, advantageous, or specific for the invention. These are the narrower and more specific claims that limit the scope of the invention. For example, some dependent claims for the device that can be fitted in a vehicle to improve the fuel efficiency of the vehicle may look like this:

The device as claimed in claim 1, wherein the sensor is a speedometer, an accelerometer, or a gyroscope. The device as claimed in claim 1 or 2, wherein the controller is a microprocessor, a microcontroller, or a digital signal processor. The device as claimed in any one of claims 1 to 3, wherein the injector is a solenoid valve, a piezoelectric valve, or a magnetic valve. The device as claimed in any one of claims 1 to 4, wherein the device further comprises a display that can show the fuel efficiency and other information to the user. The device as claimed in any one of claims 1 to 5, wherein the device is compatible with any type of vehicle, such as a 2 wheeler or a 4 wheeler.

Step 4: Review and revise the claims to ensure that they comply with the requirements and guidelines for writing claims, as well as the ethical and legal standards of patentability. Check for clarity, conciseness, support, novelty, inventive step, industrial applicability, punctuation, grammar, terminology, definitions, numbering, and order of the claims. Make sure that the claims are consistent and coherent with the detailed description and the drawings, if any.

Common Mistakes and Pitfalls to Avoid When Writing Claims

Writing claims is not an easy task, and there are many common mistakes and pitfalls that can affect the quality and validity of the claims. Some of the common mistakes and pitfalls to avoid when writing claims are:

- Using vague or ambiguous terms or expressions, such as "substantially", "approximately", "preferably", or "such as". These terms or expressions can introduce uncertainty and confusion in the interpretation and scope of the claims, and may also invite objections or rejections from the patent examiner or the courts.
- Using unnecessary or redundant features or elements, such as "means for", "adapted to", or "comprising". These features or elements can make the claims too broad or too narrow, and may also violate the principle of conciseness and support. They may also limit the scope of the claims to the specific embodiments disclosed in the detailed description or the drawings, and exclude other equivalent or alternative embodiments that fall within the scope of the invention.
- Copying or modifying the claims from the prior art or other sources. This can result in the claims being anticipated by or obvious from the prior art, and may also infringe the intellectual property rights of others. It may also lead to the claims being inconsistent or incompatible with the detailed description or the drawings, and may also introduce errors or inaccuracies in the claims.
- Drafting too many or too few claims, or claims that are too broad or too narrow. This can affect the balance and the coverage of the claims, and may also increase the complexity and the cost of the patent application. It may also expose the invention to the risk of being invalidated or infringed by others. It is advisable to draft a reasonable number of claims, and to vary the scope and the format of the claims, to cover the different aspects and embodiments of the invention.
- Ignoring or neglecting the feedback or the objections from the patent examiner or the courts. This can result in the claims being rejected or invalidated, and may also delay or prevent the grant or the enforcement of the patent. It is important to respond to the feedback or the objections from the patent examiner or the courts in a timely

and respectful manner, and to amend or clarify the claims as necessary, to overcome the issues or the challenges raised by them.

Abstract

The 'Abstract' of a patent application serves as a brief summary, providing a quick overview of the invention. Under the guidelines of the Indian Patent Manual, the abstract plays a crucial role in the patent examination process, offering a snapshot that encapsulates the essence of the invention.

Role and Purpose of the Abstract:
1. Snapshot of the Invention: The abstract offers a concise summary, allowing readers, including patent examiners and researchers, to quickly understand the fundamental nature of the invention.
2. Aid in Searches: It is used in patent databases to facilitate quick searches and identification of relevant patents.
3. Legal and Procedural Utility: In the Indian patent system, the abstract is important for administrative and procedural purposes, forming part of the public record.

Guidelines for Drafting the Abstract:
1. Conciseness: The abstract should be brief, ideally no more than 150 words, succinctly summarizing the invention.
2. Clarity: Use clear and straightforward language to describe the invention. The abstract should be understandable to individuals familiar with the field but not necessarily experts.
3. Inclusiveness: Although concise, the abstract should include the key aspects of the invention, particularly those that represent its novelty and utility.
4. Technical Information: While avoiding excessive detail, the abstract should contain enough technical information to convey the invention's purpose and how it is achieved.
5. No New Information: The abstract should not include information that is not present in the rest of the patent application.

The Abstract in the Patent Examination Process:
- During the examination process, the abstract assists examiners in quickly ascertaining the nature and scope of the invention, helping

them to determine the context and relevance of the invention in its field.
- It plays a role in preliminary searches for prior art, as examiners may use the abstract to identify potentially relevant patents and documents.

Legal Considerations as per the Indian Patent Manual:
- The abstract must be consistent with the content of the patent application, particularly the claims and the detailed description.
- It should not contain statements on the perceived value or commercial advantage of the invention.

The abstract is a critical component of a patent application, serving as a concise summary that highlights the key elements of the invention. In the context of the Indian patent system, a well-crafted abstract not only aids in the examination process but also ensures that the invention is appropriately represented in patent databases and public records. It should strike a balance between brevity and comprehensiveness, accurately reflecting the invention's novelty and utility.

For example, a good abstract for the same invention could be "A smart watch with an integrated electrocardiogram sensor that can measure and display the heart rate and rhythm of the user, and alert the user or a third party in case of any abnormality. The smart watch comprises a display unit, a processor unit, a communication unit, a power unit, and a sensor unit. The sensor unit includes an electrocardiogram sensor that is attached to the wristband of the smart watch and contacts the skin of the user. The sensor unit collects and transmits the electrocardiogram signals to the processor unit, which analyzes and displays the results on the display unit, and sends a notification to the communication unit if necessary. The smart watch provides a convenient and non-invasive way of monitoring the cardiac health of the user, and can prevent or reduce the risk of cardiac diseases and emergencies."

Here are **two examples of abstracts** of patent for different types of inventions:
- A smart watch with an integrated electrocardiogram sensor that can measure and display the heart rate and rhythm of the user, and alert the user or a third party in case of any abnormality. The smart watch

comprises a display unit, a processor unit, a communication unit, a power unit, and a sensor unit. The sensor unit includes an electrocardiogram sensor that is attached to the wristband of the smart watch and contacts the skin of the user. The sensor unit collects and transmits the electrocardiogram signals to the processor unit, which analyzes and displays the results on the display unit, and sends a notification to the communication unit if necessary. The smart watch provides a convenient and non-invasive way of monitoring the cardiac health of the user, and can prevent or reduce the risk of cardiac diseases and emergencies.

- A method for making tea, comprising the steps of boiling water in a kettle, placing tea leaves or tea bags in a teapot, pouring the boiled water over the tea leaves or tea bags in the teapot, steeping the tea leaves or tea bags in the teapot for a desired time, removing the tea leaves or tea bags from the teapot, and serving the tea in cups or mugs. The method further comprises the step of adding sugar, honey, milk, cream, lemon, or other flavorings to the tea before or after serving. The method allows the user to make tea easily and quickly, and to customize the taste and strength of the tea according to their preference.

Drawings

Patent drawings are graphical representations or diagrams that accompany a patent application to visually demonstrate the invention in question. They offer a visual guide that details the invention's unique features, how it operates, and how it could be produced. Patent drawings can depict anything from simple mechanical devices to complex technological systems, architectural structures, or intricate chemical compounds. The primary purpose of these illustrations is to make the invention easier to understand, supplementing the often technical and complex written description.

The Indian Patent Office has outlined specific guidelines for these drawings in Rule 15 of the Patents Rules, 2003. They must be clear, concise, and capable of reproduction when printed. All drawings must be in black and white, with exceptions made for color drawings if they are essential for the understanding of the invention. The drawings should be made with the assistance of a draftsman, if possible, and every feature of the invention specified in the claims must be depicted. Furthermore, reference numerals must be used to identify elements in the drawing, and these numbers should correspond with the elements described in the detailed description of the patent application.

The following are some of the main requirements and guidelines for patent drawings as per Indian patent law:

- Drawings, when furnished by the applicants otherwise than on requisition made by the Controller, shall accompany the specifications to which they relate.
- No drawings or sketch, which would require a special illustration of the specification, shall appear in the specification itself.
- At least one copy of the drawing shall be prepared neatly and clearly on a durable paper sheet.
- Drawings shall be on standard A4 size sheets with a clear margin of at least 4 cm on the top and left hand and 3 cm at the bottom and right hand of every sheet.
- Drawings shall be on a scale sufficiently large to show the inventions clearly and dimensions shall not be marked on the drawings.
- Drawings shall be sequentially or systematically numbered and shall bear in the left hand top corner the name of the applicant; in the right hand top corner, the number of the sheets of drawings, and the consecutive number of each sheet; and in the right hand bottom corner, the signature of the applicant or his agent.
- No descriptive matter shall appear on the drawings except in the flow diagrams.

Mistakes to avoid when writing a patent application

Some common mistakes to avoid when writing a patent application are:

- Failing to perform a prior art search before starting the patent drafting process. A thorough prior art search can help you identify existing patents or publications that may invalidate your invention or limit its scope. By uncovering relevant prior art, you can refine your invention's unique aspects and strengthen your patent application
- Providing an inadequate description of the invention. A detailed and comprehensive description should clearly define the technical features, functionality, and advantages of the invention. Lack of clarity or incomplete disclosure may result in a weak or unenforceable patent
- Omitting key patent claims or writing vague or inconsistent claims. Patent claims are the legal statements that define the scope and content of your patent. They determine what you can exclude others from making, using, selling, or importing. Failing to include well-crafted claims or omitting important claim elements can limit the value and enforceability of your patent. Careful consideration should be given to drafting claims that cover various embodiments and potential infringing activities.
- Using imprecise or inconsistent terminology in the patent application. Accurate and consistent use of terminology is crucial in patent drafting. Vague or inconsistent language can lead to ambiguity and potential disputes during patent examination or enforcement. It is vital to define key terms clearly and use them consistently throughout the patent application to ensure a strong and unambiguous disclosure
- Neglecting patent drawings and figures or providing unclear or inaccurate drawings. Patent drawings and figures are graphical representations of your invention that supplement and clarify the patent specification. They should be clear, detailed, and accurate, and should show the different views, aspects, and embodiments of your invention. They should also include reference signs that correspond to the elements of your invention as described in the patent specification and claims. Neglecting to include clear, detailed, and accurate drawings can weaken your patent

- Failing to identify and emphasize the novel and non-obvious features of your invention. Patentable inventions must possess novelty and non-obviousness. Neglecting to emphasize these aspects of your invention can weaken its patentability. Carefully identifying and highlighting these features in the patent application strengthens your arguments for patent approval
- Providing incomplete or inconsistent inventorship information. The issue of inventorship is critical in patent drafting. Failing to accurately identify and include all inventors can lead to disputes and potential invalidation of the patent. You should ensure that all inventors have contributed to the conception of the invention and have agreed to be named as inventors
- Mischaracterizing the results or facts of the invention or making false or misleading statements. You should avoid exaggerating or misrepresenting the results or facts of your invention or making any false or misleading statements in your patent application. Such statements can damage your credibility and expose you to legal liabilities. You should provide accurate and truthful information and support it with evidence and data
- Failing to balance the obviousness and enablement requirements. Obviousness and enablement are two important criteria for patentability. Obviousness means that your invention is not obvious to a person skilled in the art, while enablement means that your invention is sufficiently disclosed and can be made and used by a person skilled in the art. You should avoid disclosing too much or too little information in your patent application, as this can affect the obviousness and enablement of your invention. You should disclose enough information to enable your invention, but not so much that it makes your invention obvious
- Failing to comply with the patent law and practice of the country where you are filing. Different countries have different patent laws and practices, and you should be aware of the specific requirements and guidelines of the country where you are filing your patent application. Failing to comply with the patent law and practice of the country where you are filing can result in rejection, delay, or invalidation of your patent. You should consult a patent attorney or agent before filing your patent application to ensure that you meet the legal and procedural standards of the country where you are filing

7. Filing Patent application

Filing Patent application:

- Different options, paths and strategies for Filing patent application
- Provisional patent application
- When to go for provisional patent application
- advantages
- costs
- elements of provisional patent application
- mistakes to avoid
- Complete patent application
- International patent application
- different options and routes available
- strategies to go about international patent filing
- Patent Cooperation Treaty (PCT) application
- The ideal way to proceed with your invention after patent filing
- What are benefits of patent pending status?
- Patent pending status
- things you can do after filing patent
- things you cannot do till grant of patent

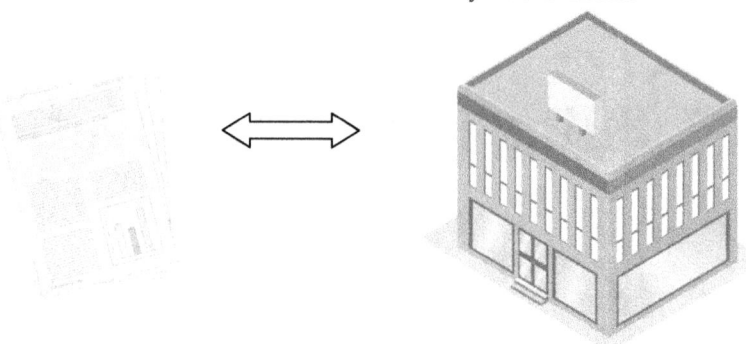

Once you and your patent attorney approves the final version of patent application it is file into the patent office as soon as possible.

there are many options and routes for filing patent application based on following things:

□ the stage of your invention
□ the country of your interest for getting patent protection
□ number of countries of your interest forgetting pattern protection outside India
□ your budget for filing patent application

Types of patent applications

1. Provisional application

a provisional application is filed when you are not quite ready with your invention and you want to borrow the time to work further on research and development of your invention and at the same time you don't want to lose on priority date. A provisional specification may or may not have claims.

Filing provisional application gives you 12 months of time within which you need to file complete patent application. If you fail to file complete patent application within 12 months from the filing of provisional patent application your application will be abandoned.

2. Complete application

The complete application / specification describes the invention fully and completely along with the best mode and complete set of claims the complete specification includes following elements:

- ☐ Title and Preamble
- ☐ Prior art
- ☐ Drawbacks in prior art
- ☐ Efforts or Solution to Drawbacks
- ☐ Summary Of the Invention
- ☐ Statement of invention
- ☐ Detail description of invention
- ☐ Detail description with reference to drawings
- ☐ Examples
- ☐ Claims

3. Convention Application

When an applicant files the application for a patent, claiming a priority date based on similar application filed in convention countries, it is called a convention application.

You can file the application in the Indian Patent Office within twelve months from the date of first filing of a similar application in the convention country.

4. Patent Cooperation Treaty (PCT) – International Application

It is an international agreement for filing patent applications having effect in up to 138 countries.

"PCT is administered by World Intellectual Property Organization WIPO, and it's primary objective is to provide a system where you need to make only one patent application which would be searched by at least one International search authority and examined by at least one selected International preliminary Examination Authority IPEA"

It is important to remember that pct does not provide the grant of patent it only facilitates single application which would be taken from searching to examination stage centrally and which would be applicable for all the signatory countries in pct. Currently number of countries associated in PCT are 138.

The application is to be filed in English language within 12 months from the date of filing in India.

5. PCT-National Phase Application

This is an application filed in Indian Patent Office claiming the priority of international filing date is called PCT National Phase application.

First the international application is made as per (PCT) and then the first application, can enter the national phase in India within 31 months from the international filing date or priority date (whichever is earlier).

Documents required for filing of A Patent Application

- Covering letter- indicating the list of documents;
- Application for Grant of Patent in Form 1 [section 7, 54 & 135 and Rule 20(1)] in duplicate;
- Complete/Provisional specification in Form 2 in duplicate [Section 10; Rule 13]
- Statement and Undertaking in Form 3 [Section 8; Rule12];
- Power of Attorney in Form 26 (in original) (Rule 3.3 (a) (ii)); (if filed through attorney)
- Declaration of Inventor-ship in Form 5 (only in case of an Indian Application; (Rule 4.17);
- Request for examination: Form 18
- Requisite Statutory fees (cheque / DD).
- Request for publication. This is optional (form 9) if express publication is required.
- Form 28 only required to be submitted by small entity

Patent co-operation treaty (PCT)

Link for video

As explained earlier patents are territorial. that means if you have patent for your invention in India you cannot stop someone from making using selling offering for sale or importing your patented invention in some other country, that is other than India.

Now obviously you want to go for as many countries as possible to protect your invention.

If you go by traditional way (that is by paris convention) you need to file patent applications in all countries of your interest within 12 months from the date of filing of patent application in your home country.

The Paris Convention is an international treaty that allows applicants to file a first application in their home country. And within 12 months period further application called a Paris Convention application could be filed at desired countries.

Now for example you selected 10 countries to file your patent application, can you imagine the simultaneous workload? doing all the steps in all the countries of your interest like replying to objections, request for examinations, translating your patent application into different languages and ultimately professional charges of patent agents and attorneys involved at different patent office... and all this happening **simultaneously** !!!

this is what would happen if you take the traditional route for international filing of your patent application. to avoid such chaotic condition expenses and additional workload **patent cooperation treaty** created.

"PCT is administered by World Intellectual Property Organization WIPO, and it's primary objective is to provide a system where you need to make only one patent application which would be searched by at least one International search authority and examined by at least one selected International preliminary Examination Authority IPEA"

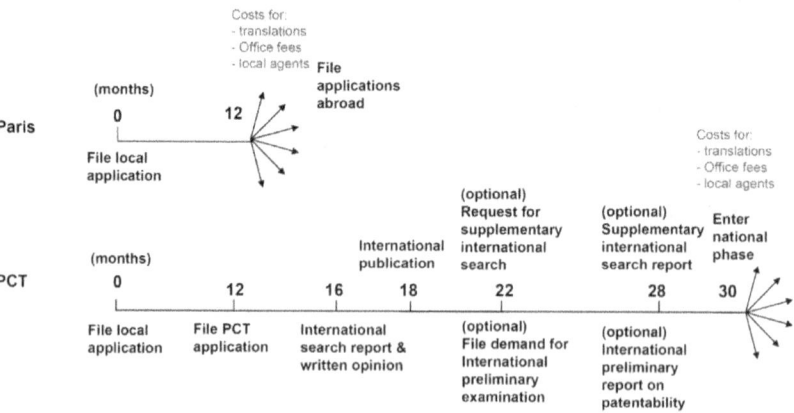

It is important to remember that pct does not provide the grant of patent it only facilitates single application which would be taken from searching to examination stage centrally and which would be applicable for all the signatory countries in pct. Currently number of countries associated in PCT are 157.

when you file International patent application to pct Unlike the previous (traditional) option, your international patent application is valid for all 157 member countries of PCT (that is up to international phase) and here you have about 30 to 31 months of time to decide whether to enter into the national phase of the country of the interest. This decision depends on the international search and examination report. India joined pct membership on 7th of December 1998.

For fees and patent professional charges for PCT (international patent filing)Refer chapter 8, "Important tables charts and references"

Advantages of PCT for International Patent application

advantages of pct application over paris convention:

□ The pct provides most effective and most economic way of filing patent application in multiple countries
□ It enables the application to file single patent application with single patent office in single language having effect in each country to pct
□ The application is searched by international search authority
□ It provides formal examination of international application by an international preliminary examination authority
□ centralized International Publication of international patent application
□ reduced load on patent officers by taking international patent application through searching and examination before entering in to the national phase

International phase is the phase during which the international patent application is published, search and examined before entry in designated country (that is national phase)

National phase is the phase when International patent application enter in the countries of interest. The international patent application is searched and examined by National patent offices and its granted or rejected

Provisional patent application

When you are at a stage in your research and development work where, it can be disclosed on paper but it's not a final invention, then you can prepare a description of the invention as provisional specification and submit to patent office to secure the priority date of the invention.

It gives following benefits:

- ✓ Secures filing date
- ✓ 12 months of time to file complete specification
- ✓ Low upfront cost

Link for video

When you complete the required documents and your research work then you can file complete specification.

Filing the provisional specification is an **optional step**, if you are at the stage where you have complete information about your invention then you can directly go for complete specification.

Important things to remember about provisional patent application:

- A provisional specification is not a rough draft;
- it defines the field of invention and also defines the scope of the invention to certain extent.
- Even if you file complete specification later it does not replace the provisional specification, it still remains in the record.
- The patent office accords the filing date and patent application number to the provisional specification received.
- If the complete specification is not filed within 12 months from the filing date of provisional specification, the patent application is treated as deemed to have been abandoned.

How filing provisional application could help?

If we see a typical life cycle of a patent owner, the most preferred way you get your ROI with the patents is by licensing it to other business. The Success in licensing your patent to other business lies in how you talk to decision makers and project the advantages and potential profits by licensing rights for your patented invention. However instead of going for complete patent, you can choose to go with provisional patent application.

Advantages of Provisional patent application

- ☐ **Low upfront cost:** you end up paying much less for filing a provisional application than filing a complete patent application.
- ☐ You can write **"Patent Pending"** status: Although provisional patent is not actually a patent and it will not be converted to complete patent application unless you take further steps... You legally can write "Patent Pending" for your invention. (product prototype) up on filing provisional patent you have secured the priority date as its filing date, so you need not worry about confidentiality.

- **Time to let invention Evolve:** Filing a complete patent application at very early stage of the invention could be a mistake and it may not protect your invention adequately, so filing provisional application secures your priority date and gives you enough time to work on your invention to the fullest possible potential.
- **Time to test the commercial potential:** Having secured the priority date by filing a provisional application, you can test few things like:
    - Willingness of other businesses to license your invention then patented
    - Get an understanding about commercial worth of invention
    - Time to conduct market research and test commercial potential
    - In effect you get full 12 months of time to decide whether to move ahead with complete patent application or not, as during this period you can do extensive market research and find the commercial worth of your invention without worrying about its confidentiality.
- **abandon the provisional patent application:** (saves you money) In case you happened to find out that the invention for which you already have filed provisional patent application is not worth going ahead for full patent protections for some reasons like:
    - The invention is not worth that much commercially
    - No one willing to buy, license it neither you willing to produce the invention, etc.

    You actually **save thousands of rupees**, you otherwise would have spent on directly going for complete patent application, and if at all decided to abandon it in between for some reasons.
- **Becomes granted Patent:** (by following procedure) the provisional patent can become granted patent if the complete patent application is filled within 12 months from filing date of provisional patent and entire patent procedure is followed till grant of patent. (Provided the patent application is not rejected by the controller)

Now, the granted patent will have the benefit of earlier priority date (that is filing date of provisional patent) as **priority date is crucially important** in all stages of patent life cycle, right from examination stage to grant of patent and even in litigations stage and even while monetizing patent.

Mistakes to avoid in Provisional Application

Be careful when writing provisional application for your invention.

- ☐ **It is a scope defining document:** A provisional application is not a rough draft of your idea or invention. In fact it defines the scope of your invention. So every part (element) of your invention which is outside the scope of the provisional application and you happened to develop in the 12 months time (that is at the time of filing complete patent application) will fail to have the earlier priority date (filing date of provisional application). Which means the part of invention you developed after filing provisional which is outside the scope which is set by provisional application will not have the advantage of priority date of provisional application.
- ☐ Even if you file complete specification later it does not replace the provisional specification, **it still remains in the record**. The patent office allocates the filing date and patent application number to the provisional application received.
- ☐ If the complete specification is not filed within 12 months from the filing date of provisional specification, the patent application is treated as deemed to have been **abandoned**.
- ☐ Another mistake would be failing to disclose the scope of invention.
- ☐ **The description of invention should not be limiting:** The language used in patent application plays an important role in defining its scope: While writing description for invention, you should avoid using limiting words like "must have" "consists" "essential" Instead try to describe elements of the invention with as broad scope as possible: You can use terms like a "writing device" instead of directly saying "a pen" which would be of limiting scope and can eliminate other writing devices like pencil from the scope.
- ☐ publically disclosing parts of invention that are not protected by provisional specification. This would destroy the novelty of the part of invention which is not covered in provisional specification

Contents of Provisional Specification

- ☐ Title of the invention
- ☐ Description of the invention starts with preamble 'The following Specification describes the invention
- ☐ The description contains
- ☐ The field of invention and containing the background of the invention
- ☐ Object of the invention and statement of the invention
- ☐ Claims may not be part of the Provisional Specification

So, in a way provisional patent application is **a way to save costs** while protecting your innovative idea meanwhile. If you utilize it in certain way, it is indeed a low upfront cost option that give you time to test the true potential of the invention before actually going for full patent procedure. additionally your **priority date is secured** and the **confidentiality** is taken care.

8. Publication of application

Generally the patent application is automatically published after 18 months from the filing date. No fees or action is required by inventor.

If you don't want to wait till the expiry of 18 months, An early publication request can be made along with prescribed fees.

Rule 24. The period for which an application for patent shall not ordinarily be open to public under sub-section (1) of section 11A shall be eighteen months from the date of filing of application or the date of priority of the application, whichever is earlier. Provided that the period within which the Controller shall publish the application in the journal shall ordinarily be one month from the date of expiry of said period, or one month from the date of request for publication under rule 24A.

Rule 24A. Request for publication.—A request for publication under sub-section
(2) of section 11A shall be made in Form 9.

The early publication request can be made (optional step) with form 9 and by paying prescribed fess as per table below; in general the patent application is published within a month form request for early publication.

		Responsibilities
Inventor		optional step of filing early publication request along with Form 9 and Fees
Patent agent or attorney		optional step of filing early publication request along with Form 9 and Fees.

Patent office		Publishing the patent application after 18 months of filing date or if requested early publication is done.

F O R M 9
THE PATENTS ACT, 1970
(39 of 1970)
&
The Patents Rules, 2003
REQUEST FOR PUBLICATION
[See section 11A(2); rule 24A]

1. Name, address and nationality of the applicant(s).

I/We[1]...

....

....

....

2. To be signed by the applicant or his authorized registered patent agent.

hereby request for early publication of my/our

Patent application No .... dated

.......................under section 11A(2) of the Act.

Dated this ....day of 20

3. Name of the natural person who has signed.

Signature ..[2]...

(--). [3]....

To
The Controller of Patents,
The Patent Office.
At ....

these is .... aths
of filing
for early   Note: - For fee : See First Schedule   o go
....

Government forms and fees:

Form 9. Remember, these is no fees for publication of application automatically after 18 months of filing date. The fees mentioned below is for optional step if you want to go for early publication request.

	Individual inventors Natural person(s) or Startup(s) or Small entit(y)/(ies) or educational institution(s)	Other(s)
Request for early publication	₹ 2500 or (USD 30)	₹ 12500 or (USD 150)

Pre-grant opposition

The Pre-Grant opposition can be filed by any person who wants to oppose the invention disclosed in our patent application. There is no fees applicable for filing pre-grant opposition.

Request for examination (RFE)

The patent application is examined only after receiving **request for examination** that is **RFE**. The inventor / applicant need to file a request for examination (RFE) within 48 months of filing date or priority date. This RFE is made with form 18 and the government fees for the same is mentioned in table below.

Up on receiving this request the controller gives your patent application to a patent examiner who performs searches for checking patentability of the invention (as per patentability criteria's). and then the examiner creates a first examination report FER of the patent application. Everything happening to patent application before grant of patent is generally called as patent prosecution. The first examination report submitted to controller by examiner generally contains prior arts (existing documents before the date of filing) which are similar to the claimed invention, and any objections raised regarding patentability requirements for the invention. Same examination report (with objections) is communicated to you (inventor) / patent applicant.

Request for examination

		Responsibilities
Inventor		patent agent or patent attorney makes request for examination with form 18 on behalf of you.
Patent agent or attorney		request for examination is submitted with Form 18 and Fees. or request for *Expedited examination with form 18 A if applicable*
Patent office		receive request for examination and examiner check patent application for patentability and other criteria and

		generates First examination report

F O R M 18 **THE PATENTS ACT, 1970** **(39 of 1970)** **&** **The Patents Rules, 2003** **REQUEST/EXPRESS REQUEST FOR EXAMINATION** **OF APPLICATION FOR PATENT** **[See section 11B and rule 20(4)(ii), 24B(1)(i)]**	**(FOR OFFICE USE ONLY)** RQ. No: Filing Date: Amount of Fee Paid: CBR No: Signature:

1. APPLICANT (S)/OTHER INTERESTED PERSON
(a) NAME :
(b) NATIONALITY :
(c) ADDRESS :
(d) date of publication of the application under section 11A ....

2. Statement in case of request for examination made by the applicant(s)

.I/We hereby request that my/our application for patent no. _____ filed on _____

for   the   invention

titled_____. shall be

examined under sections 12 and 13 of the Act.

Or

I/We hereby make an express request that my/our application for patent no. _____ filed on._

_____based   on   Patent   Cooperation   Treaty   (PCT)   application   no.

_____dated_____.

made in country _____shall be examined under sections 12 and 13 of the

Act, immediately without waiting for the expiry of 31 months as specified in rule 20(4)(ii).

3. Statement in case of request for examination made by any other interested person

I/We the interested person request for the examination of the application no. _____dated

_____filed by the applicant _____titled_____

under sections 12 and 13 of the Act.

As an evidence of my/our interest in the application for patent following documents are submitted.

(a) _____

_____

4. ADDRESS FOR SERVICE

Dated this_____ day of_____ 20

Signature
Name of the signatory

To, The Controller of Patents
   The Patent Office, at ....

NOTE:
*To be signed by the applicant(s) or by his authorized registered patent agent
*Strike out the column which is/are not applicable
* For fee : See First Schedule

Form 18

The fees for request for examination RFE is as below.

	Individual inventors Natural person(s) or Startup(s) or Small entit(y)/(ies) or educational institution(s)	Others
Request for examination	₹ 4000 or (USD 48)	₹ 20000

Request for expedited examination

This request for expedited examination is an application filed by patent applicant in Government patent office to Expedite the examination of the patent application. This request is made by using Form 18A Form 18(A) (71 KB)

Fees for expedited examination

	Individual inventors Natural person(s) or Startup(s) or Small entit(y)/(ies) or educational institution(s)	Others
Request for expedited examination	₹ 8,000 or (USD 96)	₹ 60,000 or (USD721)

Who can use such a request for expedited examination?

(a) that India has been indicated as the competent **International Searching Authority** or elected as an International Preliminary Examining Authority in the corresponding international application; or

(b) that the applicant is **a startup**; or

(c) that the applicant is **a small entity**; or

(d) that if the applicant is a natural person or in the case of joint applicants, all the applicants are natural persons, then the applicant or **at least one of the applicants is a female;** or

(e) that the applicant is a department of the **Government**; or

(f) that the applicant is an institution established by a Central, Provincial or State Act, which is owned or controlled by the Government; or

(g) that the applicant is a Government company as defined in clause (45) of section 2 of the Companies Act, 2013 (18 of 2013); or

(h) that the applicant is an institution wholly or substantially financed by the Government; or

(i) that the application pertains to a sector which is notified by the Central Government on the basis of a request from the head of a department of the Central Government.

(j) that the applicant is eligible under an arrangement for processing a patent application pursuant to an agreement between Indian Patent Office and a foreign Patent Office.

9. Examination of application

Up on receiving request for examination the controller gives your patent application to a patent examiner (generally within 1 month from publication of application or within 1 month from request for examination).

Patent examiner performs searches for checking patentability of the invention (as per patentability criteria's) and performs formal and substantive examination of the patent application. and then the examiner **creates a report on** whether
- □ application, specification and other documents are as per requirement of the patent act; and
- □ whether the invention is patentable

That report is called as a **first examination report** (FER). The first examination report submitted to controller by examiner generally contains prior arts (existing documents before the date of filing) which are similar to the claimed invention, and **any objections raised** regarding patentability requirements for the invention. Same examination report (with objections) is communicated to you (inventor) / patent applicant.

Examination of patent application

		Responsibilities
Inventor		------
Patent agent or attorney		------
Patent office		examiner check patent application for patentability and other criteria and generates First examination report

The examination of patent applications in India is a crucial step in the process of granting patents. It plays a pivotal role in ensuring that only inventions meeting the criteria of novelty, non-obviousness, and industrial applicability are granted exclusive rights. This article provides a detailed overview of the examination process for patent applications in India, highlighting the steps involved, the role of the Indian Patent Office, and the key factors considered during examination.

Examination Process for Patent Applications
1. Formal Examination: The first stage of examination is the formal examination, where the patent office reviews the application for compliance with formal requirements. This includes checking whether the application contains all the necessary documents, such as a complete specification, abstract, and drawings, and if the application fee has been paid. If any deficiencies are found, the applicant is given an opportunity to rectify them.
2. Publication of the Application: Once the formal requirements are met, the application is published in the official journal. This publication allows interested parties to examine the invention and file pre-grant oppositions if they believe the invention does not meet the patentability criteria.
3. Substantive Examination: The heart of the examination process is the

substantive examination, where the patent office assesses the invention's patentability. This involves evaluating whether the invention is novel, involves an inventive step, and is capable of industrial application. The examiner also considers the claims made in the application to determine their scope and validity.

a. Novelty: The examiner checks if the invention is new and not disclosed in any prior art, including earlier patent applications and publicly available information.

b. Inventive Step: The examiner assesses whether the invention involves an inventive step, meaning it is not obvious to a person skilled in the relevant field.

c. Industrial Applicability: The invention must be capable of being made or used in some industry.

d. Sufficiency of Disclosure: The application must provide enough information for a person skilled in the field to make or use the invention.

Examination Report: Following the substantive examination, the patent office issues an examination report. This report outlines any objections, prior art references, or deficiencies identified during the examination. The applicant is given an opportunity to respond to these objections and provide counterarguments or amendments to address the issues raised.

Amendment and Arguments: The applicant can file amendments to the application and submit arguments in response to the examination report within the prescribed timeframe, typically four months.

Further Examination and Decision: After receiving the applicant's response, the examiner conducts further examination. If the examiner is satisfied with the applicant's response and believes that the invention meets all patentability criteria, the patent is granted. If not, a hearing may be scheduled to discuss the issues further.

Grant of Patent: Once all objections are addressed and the examiner is satisfied with the application, the patent is granted, and the applicant is required to pay the grant fee. The patent is then published in the official journal.

The examination of patent applications in India is a rigorous and multi-step process designed to ensure that only deserving inventions are granted patent protection. It involves a thorough evaluation of the invention's novelty, inventive step, and industrial applicability, along with adherence to formal requirements. Through this process, the Indian Patent Office plays a crucial role in fostering innovation and protecting intellectual property rights in the country. Inventors and applicants seeking patent protection in India must navigate this process diligently to secure exclusive rights to their inventions

First Examination Report in Indian Patent

The first examination report (FER) is a crucial document that is issued by the Indian Patent Office (IPO) after examining the patent application for its patentability and compliance with the requirements of the Patents Act, 1970 and the Patents Rules, 2003. The FER contains the objections or rejections raised by the examiner, based on the prior art and the patent law, and the suggestions or amendments to overcome them. The FER also indicates the status of the patent application, whether it is accepted, refused, or pending. The FER is communicated to the applicant or his authorized agent, and is also published on the official website of the IPO.

The FER is issued by the examiner within one month from the date of reference of the application by the Controller, or within such period as may be specified by the Controller, according to Rule 24F of the Patents Rules, 2003. The FER is issued only after the patent application has been published in the official journal of the IPO, and a request for examination has been filed by the applicant or any interested person, according to Rule 24 and Rule 24C of the Patents Rules, 2003.

The FER is issued in Form 19, which has the following sections:
- Application Number: This section mentions the patent application number assigned by the IPO.
- Applicant Name: This section mentions the name and address of the applicant or applicants of the patent application.
- Title of Invention: This section mentions the title of the invention as disclosed in the patent application.
- Date of Filing: This section mentions the date of filing of the patent application, or the date of filing of the complete specification, if the patent application is filed with a provisional specification.

- Priority Date: This section mentions the date of priority claimed by the patent application, if any, based on the earlier filing of the same invention in another country or under an international treaty.
- Date of Publication: This section mentions the date of publication of the patent application in the official journal of the IPO, according to Section 11A of the Patents Act, 1970.
- Date of Request for Examination: This section mentions the date of filing of the request for examination of the patent application, by the applicant or any interested person, according to Rule 24C of the Patents Rules, 2003.
- Date of Examination: This section mentions the date of examination of the patent application by the examiner, according to Rule 24F of the Patents Rules, 2003.
- Objections/Rejections: This section contains the detailed objections or rejections raised by the examiner, based on the prior art and the patent law, and the suggestions or amendments to overcome them. The objections or rejections are categorized into the following types:
  - Formal Objections: These are the objections related to the form and format of the patent application, such as the title, abstract, drawings, claims, etc. These objections can be easily rectified by the applicant by making the necessary corrections or modifications in the patent application.
  - Substantive Objections: These are the objections related to the substance and merit of the patent application, such as the novelty, inventive step, industrial applicability, clarity, sufficiency, etc. These objections can be challenging to overcome by the applicant, as they require the applicant to provide arguments or evidence to support the patentability of the invention, or to amend the claims to distinguish the invention from the prior art.
  - Other Objections: These are the objections related to any other matter that may affect the grant of the patent, such as the disclosure of the source and geographical origin of biological material, the disclosure of the best method of performing the invention, the disclosure of the information pertaining to the corresponding foreign applications, etc. These objections can be resolved by the applicant by providing the required information or documents in the patent application.

Status of Application: This section indicates the status of the patent application, whether it is accepted, refused, or pending, based on the examination report. The status of the patent application can be one of the following:

- Accepted: This means that the patent application has been found to be in order for grant of patent, and no objections or rejections have been raised by the examiner, or the objections or rejections have been satisfactorily overcome by the applicant. The patent application will be granted by the IPO, after the expiry of the pre-grant opposition period, or after the disposal of any pre-grant opposition filed, whichever is later.
- Refused: This means that the patent application has been found to be not in order for grant of patent, and the objections or rejections have not been satisfactorily overcome by the applicant, or the applicant has failed to respond to the examination report within the prescribed time and manner. The patent application will be refused by the IPO, and the applicant will have no further right to pursue the patent application, unless he files an appeal against the refusal within the prescribed time and manner.
- Pending: This means that the patent application is still under examination, and the applicant has to submit his reply to the examination report, along with the amended application, if any, within six months from the date of communication of the report, or within such period as may be extended by the Controller, according to Rule 24G of the Patents Rules, 2003. The patent application will be further examined by the IPO, and a hearing may be conducted, if required, before granting or refusing the patent application.

The FER is a vital document that determines the fate of the patent application, and the applicant should carefully read and understand the FER, and take appropriate actions to respond to the FER, within the prescribed time and manner, to secure the grant of the patent.

The applicant may seek the assistance of a professional patent agent or attorney, who can help the applicant in drafting and filing the reply to the FER, and in representing the applicant before the IPO, if required. The FER is also a valuable source of information for the competitors and the public, who can monitor the progress and status of the patent application, and file a pre-grant opposition or representation, if they have any grounds to challenge the patentability of the invention.

Response to objections

Majority of patent applicants (inventors) will receive some type of objections based on examination report. The best thing to do it analyze the examination report with patent agent / attorney and creating a response to the objections raised in the examination report. This is a chance for an inventor to communicate his novelty and non obviousness of the invention based on the kind of objections received.

You (as inventor) / applicant supposed to answer the objection raised **within 12 months** from the date on which the First examination report is forwarded to you.

The inventor and patent agent create and send a response to the objections that tries to prove to controller that his invention is indeed patentable and satisfies all patentability criteria's. or optionally accepts the objections and amends the patent application as pointed out in First examination report. If the controller is satisfied with the response to the objections or the amended patent application. Up on finding the patent application in order of grant, The patent is granted to you (inventor) / applicant as early as possible !!! with a seal of patent office and the date of grant is registered in register of patents.

Response to objections

		Responsibilities
Inventor		help patent agent in technical matters of invention (If required) with drafting response for objections.
Patent agent or attorney		draft the response to objections raised with the help of inventor. Or amend the patent application accordingly. Request for hearing if desired.

Patent office		receive response of objections and decide whether a hearing is needed and whether to grant patent or not

Professional Fees:

The patent agent /attorney may charge a professional fees to respond to objections based on complexity of the objections and number of objections received.

The fees for response to objections varies from Rs. 15000 to Rs. 25000 depending up on complexity, subject matter and number of objections.

10. Grant of patent

The application would be placed in order for grant once it is found to be meeting all patentability requirements. The patent is granted to you (inventor) / applicant as soon as possible with the seal form patent office and The grant of patent is notified in the patent journal which is published time to time.

Grant of patent

		Responsibilities
Inventor		Patent granted to your invention. As per section *48* you get right to exclude others from using, selling offering for sale, importing your patented invention
Patent agent or attorney		Inform inventor about procedures, renewals and communication to patent office after grant of patent
Patent office		Grant the patent for invention or reject the patent based on response to objections raised. Notify grant of patent in patent journal.

Post-grant opposition

Post grant opposition may be filed at any time after the grant of patent **within one year** from the date of publication of the patent. any person interested in field of the invention can file the post grant opposition.

it is filed in the prescribed form 7 along with prescribed fees of Rs. 2400 for natural person, Rs.6000 for small entity and 12,000 for large entity.

E-filing

Particulars	Individual inventors Natural person(s) or Startup(s) or Small entit(y)/(ies) or educational institution(s)	Others
Notice of Opposition (Post-grant opposition)	2400	12000

Patent renewal

After the grant of patent, you need to maintain the patent in force or alive by paying renewal fee every year as prescribed in the schedule I.

For first two years, there is no renewal fee. The renewal fee is payable from 3rd year onwards. In case the renewal fee is not paid the patent will be cease.

Refer chapter, "Important tables charts and references" see "The First schedule"

Complete flow chart from Idea to granted patent

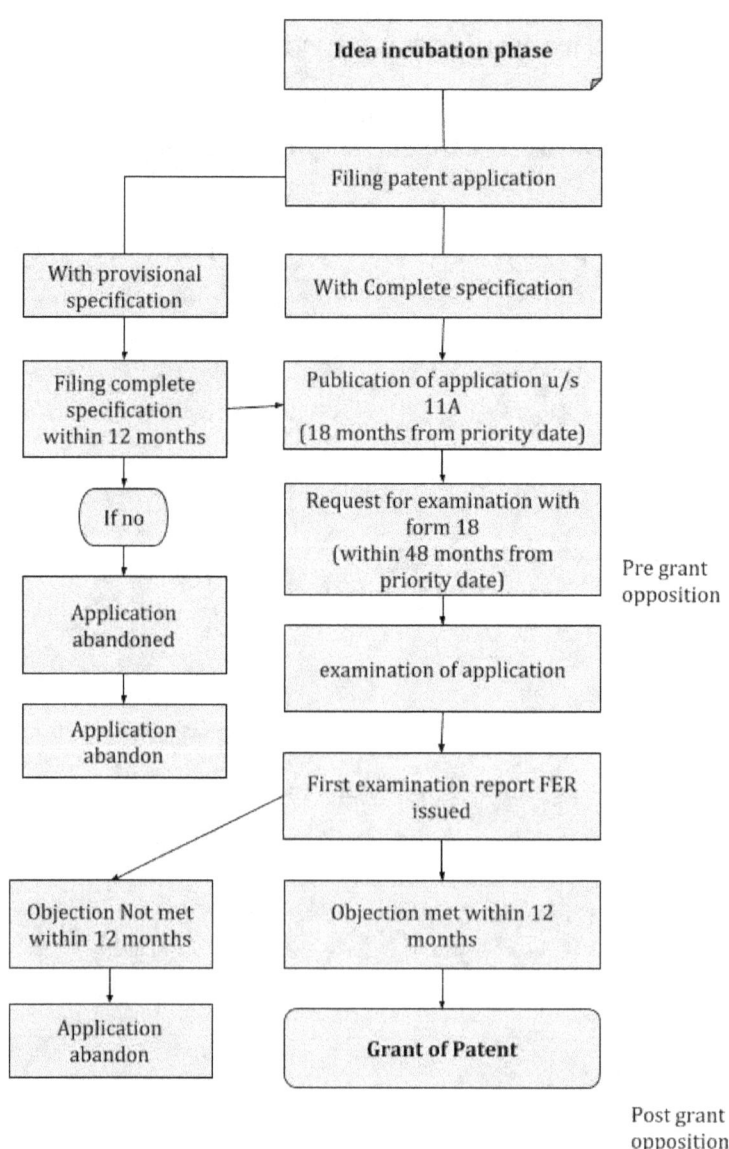

11. After Grant of patent

Grant of patent and proceedings

- Grant of patent
- What rights you can practice on grant of patent
- Different strategies to monetize your patent that is making money with your patent
- Patent infringement
- Patent enforcement
- Patent renewals
- Deciding about royalties or selling patent

Rights of a patentee

As per section 48, that is Rights of patentees: a patent granted confer upon the patentee

(a) where the subject matter of the patent is a product, the **exclusive right to prevent third parties**, who do not have his consent, from the act of making, using, offering for sale, selling or importing for those purposes that product in India;

(b) where the subject matter of the patent is a process, the **exclusive right to prevent third parties**, who do not have his consent, from the act of using that process, and from the act of using, offering for sale, selling or importing for those purposes the product obtained directly by that process in India.

Section 48 of the Act confers following rights upon the patentee (you) subject to the other provisions contained in this Act and the conditions specified in Section 47:

(a) Product Patent

Where the subject matter of the patent is a product, the exclusive right to prevent third parties, who do not have the patentee's consent, from the act of making, using, offering for sale, selling or importing for those purposes that product in India;

(b) Process Patent

Where the subject matter of the patent is a process, the exclusive right to prevent third parties, who do not have the patentee's consent, from the act of using that process, and from the act of using, offering for sale, selling or importing for those purposes the product obtained directly by that process in India.

Patent Infringement

The term **"infringement"** is not defined in the Indian statute.

As grant of patent gives exclusive right to you for excluding others from using, offering for sale, selling or importing for those purpose a patented product or a product obtained directly by a patented process or making a patented product or using a patented process within India (except for the purpose of Government use exempted under Section 47).

So performing these acts mentioned above without your (patentee's) consent are called as infringement.

In simple language, "If someone violets the rights provided to patentee by grant of patent for his invention (that is right to excluding others from using, offering for sale, selling or importing patented invention in India) then it would be called as infringement."

There are some activities which would be called as infringements:

- ☐ Government use: as per section 100 an invention can be used by central government for its own purpose.
- ☐ And as per section 47 (1), (2) the patented product may be imported by the government
- ☐ Research exemption: the use of invention for mere purpose of experiment or research including act to teaching students would not be called an infringement of patent, as there is no commercial intent involved
- ☐ Patented inventions like medicine or drug can be imported by government for its own use
- ☐ If a patented invention comes in India temporarily as a part of foreign vessel/aircraft/ vehicle then it would not be called as infringement

Filing case against infringement

As per section 104, you (patentee) can file a suit for infringement in district court or high court. But if you wish to save time you may file a suit in high court directly. As suit for infringement can be filed only after the grant of patent yet, You as a (patentee) can also **claim for damages** for the infringements that are committed between publication of patent application to the grant of patent.

Burdon of proof : If your invention is a product then the burdon of proof lies on you (patentee) that is you need to prove that the infringement has taken place. Whereas if your invention is process then burdon of proof lies on (defendant) who need to prove that he is not infringing on your patented process.

Section 108 of the Act provides the reliefs enabled in suit for infringement as follows: (1) The reliefs which a court may grant in any suit for infringement include an injunction (that is stop the infringer from pursuing the infringing activity)(subject to such terms, if any, as the court thinks fit) and, at the option of the plaintiff, **either damages or an account of profits**.

(2) The court may also order that the goods which are found to be infringing and materials and implements, the predominant use of which is in the creation of infringing goods shall be **seized, forfeited or destroyed**, as the court deems fit under the circumstances of the case without payment of any compensation.

The patent infringement in India is a violation of the exclusive rights of the patentee, as conferred by the patent. The patent infringement in India is governed by the Patents Act, 1970 and the Patents Rules, 2003, which provide the provisions, procedures, and remedies for patent infringement. The patent infringement in India can be classified into the following types:

- **Direct infringement**: Direct infringement is the most common and obvious form of patent infringement, where a third party, without the consent of the patentee, performs any of the following acts with respect to the patented invention:
    - Making, using, offering for sale, selling, or importing the patented product
    - Using the patented process, or using, offering for sale, selling, or importing the product directly obtained by that process
- **Indirect infringement**: Indirect infringement is a less apparent form of patent infringement, where a third party, without the consent of the patentee, performs any of the following acts with respect to the patented invention:
    - Inducing another person to infringe the patent, by means of supplying, suggesting, or encouraging the infringing act
    - Contributing to the infringement of the patent, by means of supplying, providing, or facilitating the infringing act
    - Willfully infringing the patent, by means of knowingly and intentionally violating the patent rights

The patent infringement in India can be proved by the patentee, by establishing the following elements:

- Validity of the patent: The patentee has to prove that the patent is valid and subsisting, and that it has not expired, lapsed, or revoked.
- Scope of the patent: The patentee has to prove that the patent covers the invention that is infringed, and that the claims of the patent define the scope and extent of the patent rights.
- Infringing act: The patentee has to prove that the infringer has performed an act that falls within the scope of the patent, and that the infringer has not obtained any license, permission, or exemption from the patentee.

The patent infringement in India can be challenged by the infringer, by

raising the following defences:
- **Invalidity of the patent**: The infringer can challenge the validity of the patent, by showing that the patent does not meet the criteria of patentability, such as novelty, inventive step, industrial applicability, disclosure, etc., or that the patent is obtained by fraud, misrepresentation, or suppression of material facts.
- **Non-infringement of the patent**: The infringer can challenge the infringement of the patent, by showing that the infringing act does not fall within the scope of the patent, or that the infringing product or process is different from the patented invention, or that the infringing product or process is covered by another patent.
- **Exemption from infringement**: The infringer can claim exemption from infringement, by showing that the infringing act is done for the following purposes:
  - Research or experimental use
  - Teaching or academic use
  - Governmental or public use
  - Importation of patented products by the patentee or his licensee
  - Parallel importation of patented products by a person duly authorized under the law
  - Bolar provision for obtaining regulatory approval
  - Use of patented invention on foreign vessels, aircrafts, or land vehicles

The patent infringement in India can be remedied by the patentee, by seeking the following reliefs:
- **Injunction**: The patentee can seek an injunction, which is an order of the court to restrain the infringer from continuing or repeating the infringing act. The injunction can be temporary or interlocutory, which is granted before the final decision of the case, or permanent, which is granted after the final decision of the case.
- **Damages or account of profits**: The patentee can seek damages or account of profits, which are monetary compensation for the loss or injury caused by the infringement. The damages are calculated based on the actual loss suffered by the patentee, or the reasonable royalty that the patentee would have received from the infringer. The account of profits are calculated based on the actual profits made by the infringer from the infringement, or the reasonable profits that the

infringer would have made from the infringement.

- **Delivery or destruction of infringing goods**: The patentee can seek the delivery or destruction of the infringing goods, which are the products or processes that embody the patented invention. The delivery or destruction of the infringing goods is done to prevent the further use or sale of the infringing goods, and to restore the market position of the patentee.
- **Other reliefs**: The patentee can seek other reliefs, such as declaration of infringement, seizure or confiscation of infringing goods, publication of the court's decision, etc., as the court may deem fit and proper.

Some of the landmark cases of patent infringement in India are as follows:

- **Bajaj Auto Limited vs. TVS Motor Company Limited**: In this case, the Supreme Court of India upheld the decision of the Madras High Court, which granted an interim injunction in favour of Bajaj Auto, restraining TVS Motor from manufacturing and selling its two-wheeler product "Flame", which allegedly infringed Bajaj Auto's patent for its digital twin spark plug ignition technology. The court held that Bajaj Auto had made out a prima facie case of infringement, and that the balance of convenience and irreparable injury were in favour of Bajaj Auto.
- **Biswanath Prasad Radhey Shyam vs. Hindustan Metal Industries (1978)**: In this case, the Supreme Court of India laid down the test for determining patent infringement, which is based on the comparison of the essential features of the patented invention and the alleged infringing product or process. The Court held that "if the alleged infringement falls within the scope of the invention covered by the claims, then the patent is infringed irrespective of the fact that the infringer may have arrived at the infringing product or process independently and by a different route."
- **F. Hoffmann-La Roche Ltd. & Anr vs. Cipla Ltd (2015)**: In this case, the Delhi High Court held that Cipla did not infringe Roche's patent for its anti-cancer drug Tarceva, which is used for the treatment of lung cancer. The Court held that Cipla's generic version of Tarceva,

which had a different polymorphic form of the same compound Erlotinib, did not fall within the scope of Roche's patent, which claimed only one polymorphic form of Erlotinib. The Court also held that Roche's patent was invalid for lack of inventive step, as the compound Erlotinib was already known in the prior art, and the polymorphic form claimed by Roche did not show any enhanced efficacy, as required by Section 3(d) of the Patents Act, 1970.

- **Bayer Corporation vs. Union of India & Ors (2014)**: In this case, the Bombay High Court upheld the grant of the first compulsory license in India to Natco Pharma for its generic version of Bayer's patented drug Nexavar, which is used for the treatment of liver and kidney cancer. The Court held that Bayer failed to satisfy the reasonable requirements of the public, failed to make the patented invention available to the public at a reasonably affordable price, and failed to work the patented invention in India, as required by Section 84 of the Patents Act, 1970, which is a provision that aims to balance the interests of the patentee and the public. The Court also held that Natco satisfied the conditions for the grant of compulsory license, such as making efforts to obtain a voluntary license, paying adequate royalty, and using the patented invention predominantly for the supply in India, as required by Section 87 and Section 90 of the Patents Act, 1970.

- **Novartis AG vs. Union of India & Ors (2013)**: In this landmark case, the Supreme Court of India upheld the rejection of the patent application filed by Novartis for its anti-cancer drug Glivec, which was a modified form of an earlier known compound Imatinib. The Court held that the patent application did not satisfy the criteria of novelty, inventive step, and enhanced efficacy, as required by Section 3(d) of the Patents Act, 1970, which is a provision that aims to prevent evergreening of patents by making minor changes to existing drugs. The Court also held that the patent application did not disclose the best method of performing the invention, as required by Section 10(4) of the Patents Act, 1970. The Court also observed that the grant of patent to Glivec would have adverse implications for the public health and the access to affordable medicines in India.

12. Making Money with my Patent

This is the moment that makes:
- all of efforts you took in research and development,
- filing patent for your invention and
- ultimately getting patent granted for your invention

worthwhile.

Now comes the golden time, to get paid for your efforts... As discussed earlier there are different ways to make money from your patented invention.

Licensing your patent to a business:

This is the way preferred by most inventor who comes from technical background and who are also owner of the patent, in this option you license your patented invention to an existing business for whom your invention would be profitable venture and after every sale made or after a fixed time interval you would be **paid royalties** for your patent.

This is most passive form of monetary benefits your would be receiving for your patent. If the company to whom you licensed your patent is significantly large and covers a wider market reach with its products or services, then after each sale (although a fraction of the cost of product) the **money made by you would spectacular** if not significant.

The terms of payment and the percentage sharing would be decided on common agreement between you (patentee) and the company (licensee)

The approach: ideal way to search for such a business for licensing is
- doing research and coming up with a list of companies who work in the field of your invention then
- scheduling a meeting with the decision makers and
- presenting them the plan about how this patented invention can be a good fit in their business and they can see significant growth in profits

the most exciting part of this deal would be the **monopoly** you and your licensee going to enjoy for your patented invention !!!

in other words, "when a business sees that licensing patented invention from you would be profitable and more over the competitors cannot compete with this product or service as it is patented... then companies would be more than willing to work with you almost every time"

Another option would be,

Selling your patented invention to a business

Most of the things discussed in licensing option are applicable here too, the difference being the payment option. Instead of paying on monthly basis or paying royalties behind every sale the company would be more keen to buyout the patent rights from you **at significant one time price.**

In such case the money offered upfront to sell the patent rights could be significant and it would be your decision whether to negotiate further or accept the offer and sell all rights to the company.

Getting funding for your invention

If you have a patent protecting your invention then investors would be more keen to listen to you, and most probably would decide to invest with you. The reason being they speculate that if the product is successful, the competitors would not be able to compete as it is protected with patent, and hence there would be fair chance that investors would make good return on their investment along with your growth.

building business around it

Another very popular way of making money with your patented invention is building business around patented invention. Or may be protecting your existing business and invention by means of patents from competition.

This path is most rewarding and most travelled by entrepreneurs and business owners... and it is more promising as well as you are in complete control and the amount of money you are going to make is not dependent on an agreement with other party or how well other party does the business after licensing..

On the other hand there are many entrepreneurs who happen to found an innovative idea while working on some problems go for patent and end up making large sums of money by leveraging patent protection.

And not to forget you can make money in one more way that is filing a suit of infringement and if it is proven in the court you would be rewarded with reliefs.

All this is applicable if your patented invention has commercial value in the market. That is the main essence of all this monetizing strategies.

The patents are as valuable as they are worth in commercial use. In other words, there has to be a commercial value for the invention that you are patenting, there need to be companies, businesses who would potentially want to use your invention and paying you royalties. Or companies who could be interested in buying out your patent if you are willing to sale it.

If this part is missing, that is your invention is does not have any commercial value then probably your patent for that invention would also be worthless.

The amount of money to be made by patenting your invention completely depends on how much commercially valuable your invention is, and your ability to commercially exploit your patented invention.

How much money can I make by patenting my invention?

One of the most common questions that every inventor has is "How much money can I make by patenting my invention?"

Although this questions comes much later in the sequence, we will address this first as this is most important question for someone who is considering filing patent for their invention or idea.

The answer to this question is not simple or straightforward, as it depends on various factors and variables, such as the type, scope, and quality of the patent, the market demand and potential of the invention, the competition and alternatives in the field, the licensing and selling strategies and negotiations, and the legal and regulatory environment and challenges.

The second thing to consider is the value of the patent in the market. The value of a patent depends on the demand and potential of the invention, the competition and alternatives in the field, and the licensing and selling strategies and negotiations.

There is **no fixed formula or method to calculate the value of a patent**, but there are some common approaches and factors that can be used, such as the cost, income, and market approaches, and the qualitative and quantitative factors.

The following table summarizes some of these approaches and factors:

Approach	Description	Example
Cost Approach	Based on the cost of developing and patenting the invention, or the cost of replacing or reproducing the invention	The value of a patent is equal to the sum of the research and development expenses, the patent filing and maintenance fees, and the opportunity cost of the time and resources invested in the invention
Income Approach	Based on the expected income or cash flow generated by the invention, or the savings or benefits derived from the invention	The value of a patent is equal to the present value of the future royalty payments, profits, or savings that the invention can produce over its remaining life
Market Approach	Based on the comparable transactions or deals of similar or related patents in the same or similar fields	The value of a patent is equal to the average or median price or royalty rate of the patents that have been licensed or sold in the same or similar fields

Factor	Description	Example
Qualitative Factor	Based on the quality and characteristics of the patent and the invention, such as the novelty, inventiveness, usefulness, scope, validity, enforceability, and marketability of the patent and the invention	A patent that has a high degree of novelty, inventiveness, and usefulness, a broad scope of protection, a strong validity and enforceability, and a high marketability and demand is likely to have a higher value than a patent that has a low degree of these factors
Quantitative Factor	Based on the quantity and magnitude of the patent and the invention, such as the number, size, and growth of the market, the market share	A patent that has a large, growing, and stable market, a high market share and penetration, a high revenue and profit

	and penetration of the invention, the revenue and profit margin of the invention, and the risk and uncertainty of the invention	margin, and a low risk and uncertainty is likely to have a higher value than a patent that has a small, shrinking, and volatile market, a low market share and penetration, a low revenue and profit margin, and a high risk and uncertainty

Using these approaches and factors, you can estimate the value of your patent in India by conducting a thorough research and analysis of your invention, your patent, your market, and your competitors.

You can also consult a patent valuation expert or use a patent valuation tool to assist you in this process. The third thing to consider is the income and return on investment from patenting your invention in India. The income and return on investment from patenting your invention depend on how you exploit your patent commercially, such as by **producing, licensing, or selling your patent**. The following table summarizes some of these options and their advantages and disadvantages:

Option	Description	Advantages	Disadvantages
Producing	Making, using, or selling your invention yourself or through your own business	- Full control and ownership of your invention and patent - Higher potential income and profit - Greater market presence and reputation	- Higher initial investment and risk - Higher operational and marketing costs - Higher legal and regulatory compliance and challenges
Licensing	Granting permission to another party to make, use, or sell your invention in	- Lower initial investment and risk - Lower operational and marketing costs - Lower legal and	- Less control and ownership of your invention and patent - Lower

	exchange for a fee or royalty	regulatory compliance and challenges - Recurring and passive income and profit	potential income and profit - Dependency and trust on the licensee - Negotiation and monitoring of the license terms and conditions
Selling	Transferring the ownership and rights of your patent to another party for a lump sum or installment payment	- Immediate and guaranteed income and profit - No further responsibility or liability for your invention and patent	- No control and ownership of your invention and patent - No future income or profit from your invention and patent - Loss of market presence and reputation

To choose the best option for exploiting your patent commercially, you need to consider your goals, resources, capabilities, and preferences. You also need to consider the market demand and potential of your invention, the competition and alternatives in the field, and the licensing and selling strategies and negotiations. You can also consult a patent licensing or selling expert or use a patent licensing or selling tool to assist you in this process.

Explaining Patent Earnings with a Mechanical Invention Example

Let's use the example of a mechanical invention - say, an innovative water-saving showerhead - to illustrate how much money can be made from patenting an invention. We'll use hypothetical values in Indian Rupees (INR) to make this more relatable.

The Invention: A water-saving showerhead that uses advanced technology to reduce water usage by 40% without compromising on water pressure.

Market Demand and Industry: The demand for eco-friendly and water-saving devices is high, especially in urban areas where water conservation is crucial. The home utilities market is competitive, but there's always room for innovative products.

Commercialization Strategy:
1. Licensing: You decide to license your patent to a large home utilities manufacturer. They agree to pay you a 5% royalty on every unit sold. Let's say the retail price of each unit is INR 2,000, and the manufacturer sells 50,000 units in a year.
   - Annual Royalty Earnings: 5% of (INR 2,000 x 50,000) = INR 5,000,000
2. Selling the Patent: An interested company offers to buy your patent for an upfront payment. You negotiate and agree on a price of INR 10,000,000.
3. Manufacturing and Selling: You set up a small business to manufacture and sell the product. Each unit costs INR 800 to produce and sells for INR 2,000. In the first year, you sell 20,000 units.
   - Profit per Unit: INR 2,000 (selling price) - INR 800 (cost price) = INR 1,200
   - Annual Profit: 20,000 units x INR 1,200 = INR 24,000,000

Patent Infringement:
You discover a competitor selling a similar product without your permission. You file a lawsuit and win a settlement of INR 3,000,000.

Total Earnings (Hypothetical):
- Licensing: INR 5,000,000/year
- Selling the Patent: INR 10,000,000 (one-time)
- Manufacturing and Selling: INR 24,000,000/year
- Infringement Settlement: INR 3,000,000 (one-time)

Other Considerations:
- Patent Costs: Filing and maintaining a patent can cost around INR 300,000 over 20 years.
- Business Expenses: If you choose to manufacture, consider production, marketing, and operational costs.

In this example, the most lucrative option seems to be manufacturing and selling the product, followed by licensing. Selling the patent offers immediate but potentially lower overall financial returns. Infringement settlements can also contribute but are unpredictable.

This scenario demonstrates how various factors like **market demand**, the industry you're in, and your commercialization strategy significantly impact your potential earnings from a patent. It's crucial to thoroughly research and plan your approach to maximize the return on your invention.

To Further, illustrate the possible income and return on investment from patenting your invention in India, let us take another **hypothetical example** of an invention that is a new and improved solar-powered water purifier.

The invention has a patent that has a broad scope of protection, a strong validity and enforceability, and a high marketability and demand. The invention has a large, growing, and stable market, a high market share and penetration, a high revenue and profit margin, and a low risk and uncertainty.

The inventor has spent 20,000 INR on developing and patenting the invention, and has obtained the patent in 15 months. The inventor has three options to exploit the patent commercially: producing, licensing, or selling the patent.

The following table summarizes the estimated income and return on investment from each option, assuming a 10% discount rate and a 20-year patent life:

Option	Income (in INR)	Return on Investment (in %)
Producing	50,000 per year x 20 years = 1,000,000	(1,000,000 - 20,000) / 20,000 x 100 = 4,900
Licensing	10% royalty x 50,000 per year x 20 years = 100,000	(100,000 - 20,000) / 20,000 x 100 = 400
Selling	200,000 lump sum	(200,000 - 20,000) / 20,000 x 100 = 900

The table shows that producing the invention has the highest income and return on investment, followed by selling the patent, and then licensing the patent.

However, this <u>does not mean that producing the invention is always the best option</u>, as it also involves the highest initial investment and risk, the highest operational and marketing costs, and the highest legal and regulatory compliance and challenges.

The inventor needs to weigh the pros and cons of each option and choose the one that suits his or her goals, resources, capabilities, and preferences. However, you should keep in mind that the actual income and return on investment may vary depending on the specific circumstances and variables of your invention, your patent, your market, and your competitors.

You should also keep in mind that patenting your invention is not only a financial decision, but also a strategic and personal decision, that requires careful research and analysis, professional and legal assistance, and constant monitoring and evaluation.

The patents are as valuable as they are worth in commercial use.

In other words, there has to be a **commercial value for the invention** that you are patenting, there need to be companies, businesses who would potentially want to use your invention and paying you royalties. Or companies who could be interested in buying out your patent if you are willing to sale it.

The amount of money to be made by patenting your invention completely depends on how much commercially valuable your invention is, and your ability to commercially exploit your patented invention.

13. Time required to File patent application (patent pending)

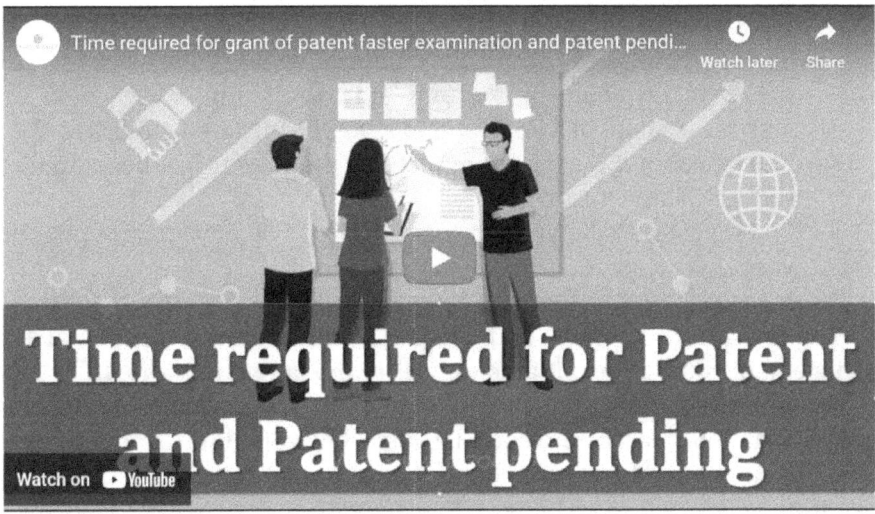

Link for video

Now, we assume that the details about your invention are ready with your and you prepared a comprehensive invention disclosure to discuss with patent agent or attorney. refer section on *Creating Final Draft of complete invention disclosure* .

from the day you start the project for patent drafting (writing) it takes about 10 to 15 days for patent agent / attorney to work on your invention and create final version of patent draft, which would be sent to you for approval and suggesting improvements if any. (time taken by you to review and respond to final version of draft adds to the total time required)

generally the patent application is filed in government patent office within 2 weeks from the start of project and **a receipt** is generated from patent office about confirmation of filing of patent application for your invention.

You can write **"patent pending"** or "patent applied" and mention the patent application number in front of your technology as soon as you file the patent application in patent office.

You can use patent pending or patent applied status for both provisional or complete patent application.

There are some subtle advantages of writing "patent pending" next to name of your product of service or may be sometimes in your resume and achievements:

- This gives an immediate impression of superior product or technology in minds of reader
- Seeing the **patent pending** or **patent applied** status, many of the competitors would be discouraged anticipating they would not be able to compete in same domain if you got granted patent
- This sends a message to public that the patent has been applied for this innovative technology
- You investors take you more seriously if you have patent pending for your invention

Having said this, there is no legal significance of these words. The infringement suit can be initiated only after the patent is granted.

The grant of patent takes more than 2 or 3 Years by normal route and within 1 or 1.5 year by expedited route . but **you don't need to wait** for grant of patent to do almost 95% of things you wanted to do with your invention:

After filing of patent application, that is receiving patent pending or patent applied status and patent application number ; you can do most of the things like:

- disclosing patented invention without fear of loosing its confidentiality (since patent is already filed and we secured the priority date already)
- testing commercial worth of invention
- demonstrating invention to other businesses or parties
- selling invention in market
- presenting information in seminar or conferences
- talking to investors or bankers for funding etc...

However, although patent pending or patent filed status has all these benefits, you **can not stop others** until you have granted patent in India (or respective country of your interest).

Time required for grant of patent in India

in this section we will see the second part of question: "Time required for getting granted patent in India"

Although there are many advantages of patent filed or patent pending states, you sometimes need to wait for grant of patent for doing some specific activity like stopping others from using your invention or to file a law suit for infringement or file a case against infringing party.

in general there are 2 timelines to consider for grant of patent.

1. time for grant of patent by Normal route
2. time for grant of patent by Expedited (Faster) route

Short Answer :

- time required for getting granted patent by normal route is more than 2 to 3 years and
- time required for getting granted patent by Expedited (Faster) route is within 1 to 1.5 years

Detailed answer:

we need to refer few sections to get complete understanding of time required considering stages involved, refer sections below

- Detailed steps and procedure for Patent
- Complete flow chart from Idea to granted patent
- Cost of filing patent in India by normal route
- Cost of filing patent in India by Expedited route

Time required for grant of patent by Normal route

Note : these are approximate time lines and may change from case to case basis.

- Novelty search : it is an optional step and time required for completing this search report is **8 to 10 days.**
- Patent drafting (writing) : time required to draft patent application is about 2 weeks that is **12 to 15 days.**
- Filing patent application : time required to file patent application upon review and approval from you (applicant) is about **1 day.**
- Publication of application : patent application is published after expiry of **18 months** from the date of filing. However you can do early publication request and it would be published within **1 month.**
- Request for Examination: we need to file request for examination RFE within 48 months from filing of patent application. sooner we file RFE the better as our application would be up in the queue of applications to be examined.
- Examination of Application and First examination report FER : it may require **more than 1 year** for your application to get examined and generate the First examination report which has objections
- Response to FER or Objection : You need to reply **within 6 months** to FER but sooner you respond with reply the better as it shortens the time required for grant. in some cases there may be need of more than one communication with government patent office as response to objections and sometimes even hearing is required. this further adds up the time required for grant of patent.
- Grant of patent : it takes more than **2 to 3 years** time for grant of patent via Normal route and this time significantly varies from case to case, number of objections received and pro activeness of applicant (you) in taking necessary steps as soon as possible

Time required for grant of patent by Expedited (Faster) route

Note : these are approximate time lines and may change from case to case basis.

- Novelty search : it is an optional step and time required for completing this search report is **8 to 10 days**.
- Patent drafting (writing) : time required to draft patent application is about 2 weeks that is **12 to 15 days.**
- Filing patent application : time required to file patent application upon review and approval from you (applicant) is about **1 day**.
- Publication of application : patent application is published after expiry of **18 months** from the date of filing. However you can do early publication request and it would be published within **1 month**.
- Request for expedited Examination: we may choose to file request for **expedited examination** for patent application. refer section on Cost of filing patent in India by Expedited route for details
- Examination of Application and First examination report FER : since **expedited examination has shorter time lines for all steps in between** we can expect the First examination report within 6 months
- Response to FER or Objection : You may choose to respond to FER as soon as possible as it shortens the time required for grant. in some cases there may be need of more than one communication with government patent office as response to objections and sometimes even hearing is required. this further adds up the time required for grant of patent.
- Grant of patent : we can expect patent to be granted within 1 to 1.5 years via expedited route and this time significantly varies from case to case, number of objections received and pro activeness of applicant (you) in taking necessary steps as soon as possible

Reduce time for grant of patent – Expedited Examination

We would compare Expedited (Faster) Route with Normal route here. Make sure you have already seen the section on Cost of filing patent in India by normal route to understand this comparison.

The grant of patent by Normal route takes **more than 2 or 3 Years.**

Although, after filing of patent application, that is receiving patent pending or patent applied status and patent application number ; you can do most of the things like:

- disclosing patented invention without fear of loosing its confidentiality (since patent is already filed and we secured the priority date already)
- testing commercial worth of invention
- demonstrating invention to other businesses or parties
- selling invention in market
- presenting information in seminar or conferences
- talking to investors or bankers for funding etc...

However, you **can not stop others** until you have granted patent in India (or respective country of your interest)

Hence sometimes you may decide not to wait for 2-3 years or even more time for grant of patent by normal route and you may decide to go for expedited (faster) route explained in detailed below.

Request for expedited examination

This request for expedited examination is an application filed by patent applicant in Government patent office to Expedite the examination of the patent application.

This request is made by using Form 18A

Request For Expedited Examination Of Application For Patent	Form 18(A) 📄 (71 KB)

Fees **for expedited examination**

	Individual inventors Natural person(s) or Startup(s) or Small entit(y)/(ies) or educational institution(s)	Large entity
Request for expedited examination	8,000	60,000

Who can use such request for expedited examination?

An expedited request can be made only by certain categories of applicants, such as:

- The applicant is a startup or a small entity
- The applicant is a female inventor or a joint inventor with a female inventor
- The applicant is a government undertaking or a joint undertaking with a government undertaking
- The applicant is eligible under an arrangement for processing a patent application pursuant to an agreement between the IPO and a foreign patent office
- The applicant has indicated or agreed to indicate India as the competent International Searching Authority or International Preliminary Examining Authority in the corresponding international application
- The applicant is a natural person or a startup and has chosen India as the International Searching Authority in the corresponding international application

Reduced time by Expedited examination

The main advantage is very short time required till grant of patent when we compare it with normal route. This benefit of requiring less time from

filing to grant (in some cases less than 1 year) is because of following things:
- The patent applications with request for expedited examination are taken on separate queue, hence would be examined much quicker than normal route
- Shorter timelines for each step along the way from filing request for expedited examination till grant of patent.

Note : in some cases the patent application is examined and First examination report can be expected within 6 months, and if you (applicant) is proactive in responding to objections and taking required steps in timely manner the patent can be granted within 1 to 1.5 year.

14. Cost of filing patent in India by normal route

The cost of getting patent depends on multiple factors.

factors which affects the total cost of getting patent in India:
- The stage of the invention (whether you are going for provisional or complete patent application)
- Route of filing patent application (Normal route, expedited route)
- Desired countries for protection of invention by patent (whether you choose India only, international patent application, PCT route or Convention route)
- Number of pages in patent application
- Number claims

- Complexity of the invention (the patent agent / attorney charges may vary here)
- Patent agent or attorney charges for drafting and filing patent application (sometimes these also defer based on type of client like individual, company or students / educational institute)
- whether or not your patent application receives objection by government patent office at the time of examination
- Response to objections (charges depending upon complexity and number of objections received by patent office)
- and many minor things may change over all cost (sometimes slightly and some times significantly)

Note: Costs discussed in the section below and subsequent chapter are exemplary and may vary with respect to patent professionals and Intellectual property firms.

What is the cost of patent registration in India?

Here is the short answer for the cost of the patent in India :
- Patent attorney fees for Patent drafting is ₹ **30,000** or (USD 360)
- Total official fees for patents by expedited (fast route) ₹ **12,100** or (USD 145) (this includes Filing fees ₹1600, Early publication ₹2500, Expedited (fast) examination ₹8000)
- **After 6 to 8 months** ;
- **If** First Examination is Received – Patent attorney fees for responding to FER is ₹ **15000** or (USD 180)
- **If** a Hearing is required with the patent office – Patent attorney charges would be ₹ **15000** or (USD 180)

Assumptions: This is assuming the applicant is a Natural person(s) or Startup(s) or Small entit(y)/(ies) or educational institution(s) and we choose to take an expedited route for a faster grant of patent hence filing early publication and expedited examination requests.

Generally speaking,

There are two elements for cost of getting patent / filing patent in India:
- The Government fees for Forms, requests and renewals.
- Professional Charges for patent professional that is patent agent / attorney

Government fees also are different for an individual inventor, small entity and a company.

link to cost sheet on government website for patent : link here

The First Schedule Fees	Fees (683 KB)

The cost for Patent in table format

Note: steps highlighted in Orange color are either optional step or depends on case to case and are not mandatory to happen

Sr.	Stages for Patent (links for more details)	Professional fees	Government Fees	Time required
1	How to go from Idea to Invention disclosure? Do I need patent agent of attorney Is my invention patentable ?	–	–	–
2	Signing Non-Disclosure Agreement (NDA)	–	–	10 minutes to sign
3	Patentability / Novelty Search (Optional step)	₹ 15,000 or (USD 180)	–	3 – 5 days
4	Drafting Complete Patent Application	₹ 30,000 or (USD 360)	–	10 – 12 days
5	Filing patent application	–	₹ 1,600 or (USD 19)	1 – 2 days
6	Publication of patent application	–	–	After 18 months
7	Early publication (Optional step)		₹ 2500 or (USD 30)	1 – 2 months
8	Request For examination (Normal Route)		₹ 4000 or (USD 48)	2-3 Years

9	Request For examination(Expedited, with a female as applicant or co-applicant,) (Optional step)		₹ 8000 or (USD 96)	8 to 9 months
10	Drafting and Filing a response to the First Examination Report (FER), In Case you receive any objection from the patent office (government)	₹ 15,000 or (USD 180)	–	Drafting response 7-10 days
11	Hearing In Case you receive any hearing from patent office (government)	₹ 15,000 or (USD 180)	–	depends on the government
12	Grant of patent or refusal	–	–	Depends on the pendency at government

Note: Government fees mentioned are for Natural persons or Startups or Small entities or educational institutions
link to cost sheet on the government website for patent: link here
The First Schedule Fees: Fees

Cost benefits for Students and academics

We all know the importance of Patent in educational environment

- The Lecturers, professors (teaching staff) are appreciated and even Promoted for getting patent for research project
- The news and media channel attention to students and institute who receives Patent for the invention
- The companies preferring students who have done research work and have patent filed or granted for the invention

we need to refer to our section on patent costs by normal route in this discussion Cost of filing patent in India by normal route

discounted attorney fees for students and educational institutes

In general patent agents / attorney offer discounted attorney fees for students and educational institutes. So, when we compare to patent filing costs with general clients, the students or educational institutes can enjoy up to 50% discounts in attorney fees. However the government or official fees for all the steps remains same.

Note: considering you are natural person(s) applicant and you filed patent application for your innovative idea or project in India, the total attorney charges for patent drafting (writing) + patent filing + request for early publication + request for examination can be as low as ₹ **20,000** in certain cases. this is without considering the official fees for relevant stages.

Discounted attorney fees for students and educational institutes as per stages

- Novelty or Patentability search (Optional step) : attorney fees ₹ 12,000
- Drafting complete patent application : attorney fees ₹ 20,000 to ₹ 25,000
- Total official fees for patents by expedited (fast route) ₹ **12,100** or (USD 145) (this includes Filing fees ₹1600, Early publication ₹2500, Expedited (fast) examination ₹8000)
- **After 6 to 8 months** ;
- If First Examination is Received – Patent attorney fees for responding to FER is ₹ **12000** or (USD 180)
- If a Hearing is required with the patent office – Patent attorney charges would be ₹ **12000** or (USD 180)

15. Answers to some important questions

What how why when: Answers to important questions

- When is the right time to file a patent application
- Patent Pending status and its advantages
- I am in research and development is patent relevant for me?
- Patent Pending or Patent filed status and its advantages
- What qualifies for a startup ?

When is the right time to file a patent application

Ideally the time to file patent application is as soon as possible there are few reasons to consider:

1. India follows first to file approach for patent system
2. to secure the priority date for patent application as early as possible filing patent application as early as possible helps in minimizing the possibility of prior arts, since more time you will take to file patent application chances are that would be more and more possible prior arts available to public.
3. if you significantly delay the patent filing process even your own work could become a prior art and hence can stop you from getting your invention patented
4. if you are working on invention which has very heavy competition and many players in the market are doing research and development in the same field, then you should file patent application as soon as possible.

How to hire right patent attorney in India : steps and selection criteria's

Link to video

If you are still confused whether you would end up saving few thousands of Rupees by writing and filing your patent application on your own (without help of patent attorney) you can read section in this book on "do I really need a patent agent / attorney ?"

In this section, we will learn some important points to consider when selecting a patent attorney based on the subject matter of your invention.

Now the next question is;

Out of thousands if not hundreds of patent agents and attorneys in India, How would I find the right one for my invention? and importantly at right costs?

Selection process for right patent attorney could turn out more complex process than you would initially imagine. Even though Google search is there to help with your decision making, yet as they say "all shining objects are not gold"

You may find most websites sound similar and it is quite difficult to differentiate patent attorney with regards to superior quality.

This problem is more intense for first time inventors (who have not filed the patent before) who are searching for a good patent attorney and **not specifically knowing what to look for** when selecting right patent attorney for protecting their invention in India.

Selecting a right patent attorney is significantly expensive decision that you are going to make and you would not want to be making mistakes in it.

Hence it is wise to be prepared. As you might have guessed, Good reputation and experience in dealing with patents from field of your invention is primary short listing factor and you can get to a shortlisted list of patent attorneys:

Does patent Attorney have degree in your field of invention?

Whatever the patent attorneys are from a science or engineering background, their degree should match with the field of your invention. This is for obvious reasons like familiarity with the subject matter of the invention. Although **this is not always necessary**, as with the experience of writing hundreds and thousands of patents from different domains a patent attorney can build a decent understanding of most related fields from different domains like electrical engineering, instrumentation, automation, technology, software engineering, etc...

Hence, although not a strict selection criteria' still as long as possible a patent attorney should have a degree from your field of the invention (or at least in nearby domains).

Personal visit or online meeting with patent agent / attorney:
Ideally it is recommended to have a short call / online meeting / visit shortlisted patent attorneys as a primary meeting and get a sense of proceedings by meeting one on one; there are advantages to in person meeting before selecting a professional.

Short listing calls to attorneys:
If the list of shortlisted patent attorneys is longer and you are unable to distinguish between them with the help of their online profiles It's better to further shortlist them by scheduling a short phone call (5 to 10 minutes) with the patent attorney who is going to work on your invention.

The some of the things to discuss in call or meeting would be:
- systems or process they follow for taking new client invention disclosure to granted patent
- cost estimate for proceeding with your patent requirement
- what in included and what is not included in the cost estimate shared
- Ask for previous work (granted patents) in same field of your invention:
- The previous work reveals too many things about quality of research and drafting for patents on which the attorney already worked on, like
- granted patents
- novelty search reports and
- responses to office actions
- any other relevant work samples from your field of invention

You can visualize your end results comparing to previous work shared by the patent attorneys in communication.

Honestly disclosing real results for novelty search:
This is another factor needed to be considered as in some cases the novelty search for the invention disclosure provided is not performed with adequate quality and attention to ensure positive opinion of patentability... so that a client (applicant) moves ahead with drafting and filing of the patent application.

Although this unethical practice is rare, it is however best avoided if patent attorney appoints an independent patent research expert for performing novelty search and provides honest patentability opinion.

How is your comfort level when communicating with patent attorney?

This is to be decided on more of a gut feeling but nevertheless this is still important factor in selecting right patent attorney to work on your invention. An in person first visit with patent attorney / agent really helps in coming conclusion with this question. Have your own thoughts and opinion and trust on your gut feeling as once selected, you are likely to work with him for years to come, even after grant of patent. Now regarding making decision based on Patent attorney charges, below is the most common question in minds of inventor

Shall I go for most expensive patent attorney or most economic one?

hiring right patent attorney

Cost for getting patent for your invention in India depends on the attorney you choose to work with. After all, your patent agent / attorney is the only ally who will **fight alongside you**:

- first for getting a patent (fight with patent office) and
- later in case of infringement of your patent, will fight with the infringing party.

Patent attorneys charges typically vary with their **expertise and experience**, highly experienced patent professional charge the highest amounts, and you probably do not need the highest possible patent professional in India to work on your invention as it could be super expensive.

Having said that, you also don't want to be working with really inexperienced patent attorney who is just starting out or who will charge ridiculously low fees compared to other patent attorneys.

In such cases you are at the risk of losing entire efforts you put in research and development along with the rights on your invention if it is not well written and not protected with appropriate claims...

"Ideal case would be patent attorney with **moderate charges and significant experience in your field of invention** who can give justice to your efforts and protect your invention to fullest possible extent."

If you happened to make a mistake, be sure that you are selecting higher side of the costing… rather than selecting an attorney with lowest possible charges…

This is because, **you still will be on winning side** even if you choose slightly highly charged patent attorney as he will ensure that your invention would be appropriately protected !!! and you do not end up losing rights on your invention due to poor quality of patent application. Or end up with granted patent which has claims that do not provide adequate protection to your invention and hence fail to monetize the patent.

I am in research and development is patent relevant for me?

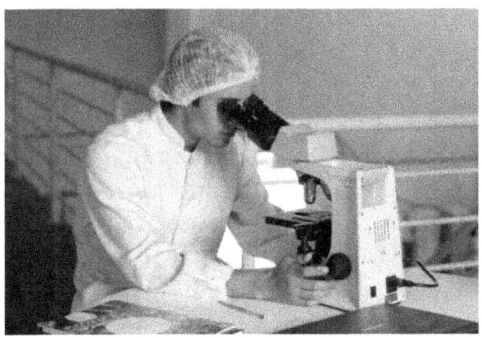

As a research and development person, you need to be very careful that you are not putting all of your efforts in something which is already invented and patented. If that becomes the case, you would be **re-inventing wheel** and probably all your research efforts are not going to be worth whole a lot

Having said that, we have also seen many people working on particular invention getting discouraged up on finding hundreds and thousands of patent from their domain and similar to their technology. This could also be a mistake.

We have a section in this book for when to get encouraged and when to get discouraged base on the results of the preliminary search conducted in chapter "Idea incubation phase"

Getting patent for an invention does not always requires and invention to be something earth breaking solution, but many patents are awarded for incremental inventions, that means most of the part of the invention would already be known to public but a small (but significant) part which is called as **'inventive step'** is the novel and non obvious part that could win patent for your invention.

As we have seen earlier in the chapter a "inventive step means" inventions that are either technically advance or economically significant to the existing patents (or prior art)

So, a prior art documents or patents that are already existing can be 95% similar to your invention Yet, if your invention has either technical advance or economic significance or both... and you can prove it that your invention is better than existing ones then there is a strong possibility that you may get patent for your invention.

The best way to take this judgment is get help from patent professional, The novelty search (also called as patentability search) is performed for the same reason, this patentability search, done right, can yield pretty fantastic results for your invention;

- It can tell you what part of your invention is already covered and what could be novelty feature...
- it can tell you where you can focus you research work to get maximum level of protection with you patent
- and it gives a review about whether it is appropriate to proceed with patent filing process

Patent Pending or Patent filed status and its advantages

You can write **"patent pending"** or "patent applied" and mention the patent application number in front of your technology as soon as you file the patent application in patent office. generally the time required for preparing and filing patent application is 10 to 15 days... hence you can get patent pending status for your invention within 15 days which has many benefits.

You can use patent pending or patent applied status for both provisional or complete patent application.

There are some subtle advantages of writing "patent pending" next to name of your product of service or may be sometimes in your resume and achievements:

- This gives an immediate impression of superior product or technology in minds of reader
- Seeing the **patent pending** or **patent applied** status, many of the competitors would be discouraged anticipating they would not be able to compete in same domain if you got granted patent
- This sends a message to public that the patent has been applied for this innovative technology
- You investors take you more seriously if you have patent pending for your invention

You don't need to wait for grant of patent to do almost 95% of things you wanted to do with your invention:

After filing of patent application, that is receiving patent pending or patent applied status and patent application number ; you can do most of the things like:

- disclosing patented invention without fear of losing its confidentiality (since patent is already filed and we secured the priority date already)
- testing commercial worth of invention
- demonstrating invention to other businesses or parties
- selling invention in market
- presenting information in seminar or conferences
- talking to investors or bankers for funding etc...

However, although patent pending or patent filed status has all these benefits, you **can not stop others** until you have granted patent in India (or respective country of your interest).

What qualifies for a startup ?

The Department for Promotion of Industry and Internal Trade (DPIIT) is a department under the Ministry of Commerce and Industry of the Government of India, which is responsible for the formulation and implementation of policies and schemes related to industrial development, trade, and investment.

The DPIIT also administers the Startup India initiative, which is a flagship program launched by the Prime Minister of India in 2016, to promote and support entrepreneurship and innovation in the country.

Under the Startup India initiative, eligible companies can get recognised as Startups by DPIIT, in order to access a host of benefits, such as tax exemptions, easier compliance, intellectual property rights (IPR) fast-tracking, funding support, and more.

To get recognized as a Startup by DPIIT, a company must meet the following criteria:
- The company should be incorporated as a private limited company, a registered partnership firm, or a limited liability partnership in India.
- The company should not have been formed by splitting up or reconstructing an existing business.

- The company should have been in existence and operation for not more than 10 years from the date of incorporation or registration.
- The company should have an annual turnover not exceeding Rs. 100 crore for any of the financial years since its incorporation or registration.
- The company should work towards the development or improvement of a product, process, or service that is innovative, scalable, and has a potential for wealth creation and employment generation.

To apply for recognition as a Startup by DPIIT, a company must follow the following steps:

- Visit the official website of Startup India at this link and register as a user by providing the basic details and verifying the email and mobile number.
- Log in to the website and fill up the online application form for recognition as a Startup by DPIIT, by providing the details of the company, such as the name, address, date of incorporation or registration, PAN, GSTIN, etc.
- Upload the required documents, such as the certificate of incorporation or registration, the memorandum of association or partnership deed, the board resolution or partner's resolution, the pitch deck or presentation, etc.
- Submit the online application form and wait for the confirmation email from the DPIIT.

The DPIIT will review the online application form and the documents submitted by the company, and will either approve or reject the application within a period of **7 working days**. If the application is approved, the DPIIT will issue a certificate of recognition as a Startup by DPIIT, which will be valid for a period of 10 years from the date of incorporation or registration of the company, or until the company crosses the turnover limit of Rs. 100 crore, whichever is earlier.

The advantage of getting recognized as a Startup by DPIIT is The company can also benefit from the faster and cheaper processing of IPR applications, such as patents, trademarks, and designs, which allows the company to avail the rebate of 80% on the patent fees, 50% on the trademark fees, and 50% on the design fees, and to get the assistance of the facilitators appointed by the DPIIT, who will provide guidance and support to the company for the preparation and filing of the IPR applications, and will also bear the costs of the statutory fees.

Conclusion Letter to Readers

Dear Valued Reader,

As we reach the conclusion of this journey, I hope this book has been a valuable guide in transforming your ideas into successful patents and ultimately into profitable ventures. From the initial stages of nurturing an idea to the exciting moment of receiving your patent grant and finally to making significant profits from your invention, this book aimed to be your companion.

We've covered a lot of ground together. You've learned about the intricacies of the patent process, the importance of protecting your intellectual property, and the strategies for monetizing your patent. The journey from an idea to a patent can be complex and challenging, but I trust that this book has simplified these concepts and given you the tools and confidence to navigate this path.

Every great invention starts with an idea and the journey from that idea to a granted patent is both rewarding and demanding. Your creativity and innovation have the power to bring significant change and success.

As you move forward from idea to invention disclosure to a granted patent, and as you venture into making profits from your endeavors, I wish you all the success in the world. Your journey is just beginning, and the possibilities are endless.

Please remember, I am always here to help. If you have any questions or need assistance along your journey, do not hesitate to reach out. Your success is important to me and I would be delighted to offer any support you might need.

Best wishes for your future inventions and innovations. May your creativity and hard work bring you great success and fulfillment.

Warm regards,

Prasad Karhad

About the author

Prasad Karhad

- Founder and Director of Patent Attorney Worldwide Private Limited
- Registered Patent Agent (IN/PA 2352), Indian Patent Office, Govt. of India
- Patent Facilitator for Start-ups, Startup India Govt. of India
- Bachelor's degree in Electronics and Telecommunication engineering.
- Author of multiple books on Patents and IPR which are included in syllabus of Many universities, and educational Institutions as a text book and reference books.
- Successfully helped 1800+ clients from 15+ years including Individuals, Entrepreneurs and Educational Institutes in the protection of Intellectual Property Rights (IPR) including Patents, Trademarks, Designs & Copyrights.

India Phone 1 : +91 1140747295
India Phone 2 : +91 8047486141
US number : +1 9179059041
Mobile number : +91 8975533075
Email: prasad@patentattorneyworldwide.com

www.ingramcontent.com/pod-product-compliance
Lightning Source LLC
Chambersburg PA
CBHW071301220526
45468CB00001B/222